SOUL THERAPY

SOUL
THERAPY

*The Art and Craft
of Caring Conversations*

THOMAS MOORE

HarperOne
An Imprint of HarperCollinsPublishers

HarperCollins books may be purchased for educational, business, or sales promotional use. For information, please email the Special Markets Department at SPsales@harpercollins.com.

FIRST HARPERCOLLINS PAPERBACK EDITION PUBLISHED IN 2022

Designed by Bonni Leon-Berman

Library of Congress Cataloging-in-Publication Data is available upon request.

ISBN 978-0-06-307144-5

22 23 24 25 26   LSC   10 9 8 7 6 5 4 3 2 1

CONTENTS

CONTENTS

INTRODUCTION

It's a simple fact: life is difficult and imperfect. Everyone has tragedies, losses, anxieties, and relationship issues. And so there are moments in most lives when it would be a great help to have someone to talk to about our troubles. Maybe everyone should be in therapy, at least at certain pressing times in life. Psychotherapy is an excellent profession, but sometimes just talking to a close friend, a spiritual guide, or a family member can help. Therapy in a general sense can go on anywhere and take many different forms.

I have been a psychotherapist for several decades and have had the honor of being intimately involved with people as they struggle with seemingly impossible issues. I have learned that being a therapist is different from doing therapy. It's not just a job or a skill but a way of being in the world. All day long and every day you learn to have a caring attitude, to listen closely, and to see beneath the surface.

It takes good ideas and an open heart to do therapy well. You are the main instrument of the work, and you can never stop learning about how human beings operate and who you are. You become a therapist first through self-discovery and then by learning how human life in general works. I feel that every hour of therapy I do teaches me and leads me further in my training. It's a kind of learning that never ends, because human beings are infinitely complex.

This is a book for both therapists and the ordinary person wanting to offer comfort and an attentive ear to a friend or relative. We are all therapists at times, and it would be helpful for the average person to know how to counsel another person well. For therapists, I hope this book deepens your work.

Therapists and "Therapists"

Some people are therapists professionally. They have university degrees, licenses, and credentials. They have offices and big chairs and some even the classic couch. They talk the jargon and often appear to have no troubles of their own.

I'm teasing a little here, because I love therapists. I think they are lucky to have the best profession there is, helping people deal with crises and conflicts. I have taught them and consider many of them my good friends.

But I also know many "therapists." The quotation marks are important, because they take the word out of its literal meaning. Sometimes you get a phone call from a relative asking if you would have a private conversation about something he is struggling with, maybe difficulty in a marriage or a serious illness. Or you may be a manager in a company and an employee is having trouble with her children or drinking too much or needs some vocational guidance.

You may be a minister or rabbi and people come to you for counseling even though you have never had formal training. You contact the "therapist" in you and offer your care and concern.

I define *therapy* as "care of the soul." In this sense therapy happens in all places all the time. And this is real therapy—caring, helpful, generous listening and responding. It is not the expert probing of a life for meaningful patterns and influential parental figures, say—that's the work of professional therapists—but it can be effective and critically important nonetheless.

When I teach therapists, I realize that they are people, too. They come to me as a teacher for care of their souls and for deeper and more meaningful ways of doing their work. So I don't see a thick wall between therapist and client. They are both persons trying to make sense of life's intricacies.

I usually recommend to therapists that they use friendship as the underlying dynamic of their work. I don't mean they should become literal friends with their clients but that the spirit underlying the relationship could be friendship. That means that the lay or amateur "therapist" is really doing therapy of a sort when they listen closely to their friend in distress. The lay therapist has much to learn from the professional, and the professional can learn from the layperson.

In this book, then, I speak to both the professional and the ordinary person. At times I turn toward one or the other, but overall I think they can learn from each other, from the spirit and manner of both ways of relating. I write directly, for the most part without jargon. But I do think the amateur could benefit from some deeper and more technical explorations of psychological terms like *transference* and *complex*. If you're learning how to be a power user with your computer or smartphone, you have to become acquainted with technical concepts. To do good therapy in the lay sense it wouldn't hurt to know some psychology.

The Platonic Therapist

My background for therapy includes Jungian and archetypal psychology, studies in religions and spiritual traditions, the arts, and even practical philosophy. When I teach therapists, I add to their professional training ideas and skills that are spiritual and philosophical. Therapy is not a new concept. Plato, the Greek philosopher who lived in the fourth century BC, wrote about the soul and often used the word *therapy*, which he defined as daily care and service. The word *psychotherapy* literally means "soul care."

So I suggest letting go of any idea that you have to solve your friend's or your client's problems and instead think of therapy as care and service. The caring friend can learn from the professional how to listen, speak, and comport herself. What the therapist learns in her training is relevant to the average person, both for her own life and for helping others. Ordinary people tend to give advice, which is more about them than the person they want to help. They often fail to separate their own lives and values from the person they are talking to. The amateur can also get caught in powerful emotional complexes and end up keeping the friend stuck in the pattern that has caused him trouble. I'm not suggesting that you pretend to be a professional therapist but that you dip into your own experience, find some wisdom, and listen closely to what your friend has to say. That is therapy as care of the soul.

For almost twenty years I taught psychiatrists, doctors, social workers, and psychologists who came to the New England Educational Institute on Cape Cod for their required continuing education credits. My purpose was to deepen their perspective through my studies on soul and my background in spirituality. In my youth I was a Catholic monk for twelve years and learned spiritual techniques firsthand and in depth. Then I studied C. G. Jung's works thoroughly and have taught at Jung societies in many places. Later, I will describe my work in the archetypal psychology originated by my friend James Hillman. In those summer sessions I found that professionals generally had a good education and training, but they had little exposure to depth psychology and the world's spiritual traditions.

My approach to therapy, rooted in a more philosophical and spiritual psychology, is particularly suited both to the professional who wants to go beyond medications and behavior changes as well as to the ordinary person who feels called to help friends and relatives when life gets complicated. Some people know that deep down they have a knack for listening and offering insights to their friends, a calling to an informal but deeply satisfying intimacy with others. The depth of this way of understanding therapy narrows the gap between the professional and the lay "soul guide."

In their training, therapists learn that common sense is not always useful in counseling others. Human life is full of paradoxes and contradictions. Trained therapists are usually good at spotting hidden patterns, while nontrained laypeople tend to use simple logic. For example, a local therapist recently appeared on television to help people deal with anxiety. First, she said, you have to acknowledge your fear, and then you can search out some comfort. This is a basic strategy for a therapist, but a nonprofessional therapist might skip the acknowledgment part and just go for the comforting.

Ideally, you could imagine a therapeutic world in which all conversations and utterances, public and private, were aimed at caring for the soul. Therefore, my ultimate goal is to recommend and sketch out a therapeutic way of life for all.

Anam Cara

When an ordinary person helps someone at a difficult moment, he is being what the Irish call *anam cara*, a soul friend. This is not simple friendship but a special one in which one person really helps and guides the other. Most of us don't have a name for that kind of friendship. The word *psychotherapy*, with its deeper meaning of "soul care," is very close, although the connotation today is too professional and out of reach of the untrained lay therapist.

This is an important point for the informal "therapist."

What you are doing for your friend is a step beyond ordinary friendship. It is a special relation of both closeness and guidance. You can sense the difference between having a conversation about sports or travel and sorting through significant relationships and career issues. You have moved from plain friendship to *anam cara*. You have added a therapeutic element that is clearly not professional but is serious.

No doubt, someone in your family or among your friends has asked for help with a personal issue. How have you felt? My guess is that you wanted to be of assistance but were not sure what to say or do. You probably did your best, but I'd like to give you some guidance in how to handle those situations well.

In the book I often speak to the professional psychotherapist, but almost everything I say holds true for anyone helping a friend or relative. All you have to do is remember that you really are a therapist, not in a professional way but seriously nevertheless.

It's not a bad idea to know the basics of how to listen well and how to talk.

For the professional, you have probably had a good education, supervised training, and extensive experience. But you may feel that your approach fails to address questions of meaning and purpose. The spiritual dimension may seem outside your expertise and yet the questions come up. I hope that you find both transcendence and depth in this book. We will discuss the search for meaning and ways in which spirit and soul interact.

I dip into a few favorite sources frequently. The *Tao Te Ching* is one of the main guides for my own life. I trust its appreciation for paradox and nonheroic action. It would be a good idea for you to read this honored text in a good translation while reading my book.* Here is a typical passage:

*The sage guides his people
By putting himself last.
Desiring nothing for himself,
He knows how to channel desires.
And is it not because he wants nothing
That he is able to achieve everything?*

I also quote C. G. Jung extensively. As I wrote this book I reread passages from Jung I have been reading all my life and found them full of insights. I suggest that you read him, too, not for his psychological system as much as for the depth of his practical knowledge. Finally, I often quote James Hillman, who was my good friend and from whom I learned a world of insights. He keenly reimagined everything he looked at, and for that I regard him as one of our greatest psychological writers. I also draw on Carl Rogers and Ervin Yalom for their humanistic approach to care and for the honesty with which they talk about their own experience as therapists. I also close each chapter with a poem to provide a new angle by which to reflect on the topic's themes.

---

*There are many good translations of the text by Lao Tsu available. I'll mention three that I use: *Tao Te Ching: A New English Version*, translated by Stephen Mitchell; *Lao Tsu: Tao Te Ching*, translated by Gia-fu Geng and Jane English; *Tao Te Ching*, translated by David Hinton.

At a time when psychology is shifting toward its scientific side, I'd like to bring back its philosophical, artistic, and spiritual roots, and I want to show how we are all often psychotherapists, especially in the etymological meaning of the soul—soul care—offering each other simple guidance and support. If ever the world needed good therapists and therapeutically sophisticated laypeople, it needs them now.

Part 1

THE MATERIAL

When you get to be older, and the concerns of the day have all been attended to, and you turn to the inner life—well, if you don't know where it is or what it is, you'll be sorry.

—*Joseph Campbell (1988, p. 3)*

Transforming events into a narrative provides a theme, direction, emotion, and insight. Therapy wants to achieve a story and to use stories from life. Add dreams and you have the material you need to glimpse the soul and begin therapy of the psyche, or psychotherapy.

Chapter 1

THERAPY AS CARE

There is an old story about an elephant and a dog who were great friends. The dog would curl up on the end of the elephant's trunk and sleep, and then sometimes the elephant would let the dog climb up on his back and ride to places the dog himself could not get to.

One day a man came along and saw the happy dog, offered the dog's owner a large sum of money, and took him away. Immediately the elephant went into a deep funk and would not eat. He lost weight and began to look ill. His trainer got worried and called in a vet, who told him the elephant was in perfect health but seemed lonely.

The trainer knew about the odd friendship of the elephant and dog and made inquiries about the dog's new owner. After extensive investigating, he found the owner, paid the man what he wanted, and returned the dog to the elephant, who seemed overjoyed. The big animal placed the dog on his head and appeared to do a dance, as only elephants can do. After that he began to eat again and regained his health.

This is a story about therapy. As I tell it, the dog is the elephant's therapist, and all he has to do to keep the elephant from being depressed is be himself and enjoy his friend. That in itself is a good lesson for therapists. I could have told the story from the point of view of the dog. He was probably also sad and not so healthy in the home of a new owner and apart from his friend. So their friendship is mutual therapy, one keeping the other healthy. Later we'll explore how a therapist benefits from doing therapy and how friendship is the most important means of bringing soul to life.

The Meaning of *Therapy*

Therapy is not a new invention. The Greek philosopher Plato, who lived twenty-three hundred years ago, defined therapy as "service" and used the word *therapeia* many times in his writings. You also find the word used forty-seven times in the New Testament, often translated into English as "heal." The older meanings, "serve" or "care for," would probably be more accurate. In Plato's dialogue *Euthyphro*, the student asks Socrates, Plato's alter ego, the meaning of "therapy." Socrates compares therapy to a farmer taking care of his horse. A farmer, of course, feeds the horse, gives it water, brushes it down, cleans its stable, and lets it out for exercise. This daily, simple, ordinary care is the basic meaning of the word *therapy*. *Psychotherapy* is psyche-therapy, care of the soul in daily life. We tend the soul with as much solicitude, daily attention, and love as a farmer takes care of his horse.

I had Plato in mind when, many years ago now, I wrote *Care of the Soul*. I thought of it as simple, daily concrete care for our essence, our depth, and the source of our humanity. If you care for your soul, you will be more human, able to relate better and find your way through life, discovering your purpose and calling. Care of the soul is not always about dealing directly with problems but solving them indirectly by discovering your deepest self and making a beautiful life.

People often think of therapy as figuring themselves out and trying to get it right. The older meaning is more concrete and ordinary. You take care of your home, your family, your animals, do work that satisfies you, play often, and spend time with friends. In the older sense, this is what therapy is about, and so it would be good for both the professional and amateur to be less analytical and more observant.

As we will see later in the book, soul care is also care for the world—other people, society, and even the things that are part of daily life. You can't very well live a soulful life in a soulless world. Sometimes, of course, when the world is in bad shape you have to do your best, but then you focus on your small world, giving it soul, and on making the greater world a place that is emotionally healthy and capable of loving connections.

The Beauty of Imperfection

Psychotherapy does not always aim at improving a person's situation or solving a problem. The soul may benefit from sadness, for example. Sometimes, when you're feeling wrecked, you may need to stay home in bed on a day when you should be at work. Care of the soul does not mean becoming a better person or being free of neurotic tendencies. It means that you open your heart and care for your soul and your world, including friends and family members.

Your soul needs daily nourishment of a special kind—friendship, creative work, community, good dining, conversation, humor, a spiritual perspective. If you give your soul what it needs and wants, your life and maybe even your physical health will likely be good. Therefore, often the best healing of life and body is serious, positive attention to the needs of your soul.

When someone comes into my consulting room for therapy, I'm on the alert for signs of the soul's condition. I will hear many stories and some complaints about life, but I see my job as caring for the deep and usually hidden life of the soul. This orientation is essential. You can't do real psychotherapy without it. Often what is called therapy looks more like life management than soul care. You can rearrange your life, but that is not the same as giving your deep soul what it needs and craves.

What are the things that disturb the soul? Doing work you don't love. Being overwhelmed by the family neuroses, which can be traced back generations. Doing too much so that your friendships suffer. Working so hard that you don't have enough play and humor in your life. Dealing with a difficult marriage or relationship. Being convinced by a church authority or your family tradition that you should not be sexual. Having been abused sexually or physically, to some degree or another, earlier in life.

The soul can be wounded, but it is so vast and deep that you can work through the wounds that affect almost everyone. You can even use them for strength and understanding. Certain wounds will always be present, but you can go on with a creative and satisfying life that over time deals with the wounds.

These matters I am describing now, such as the emotional wounds and family neuroses, demand special attention, and that is where the professional can offer valuable care and understanding. Professional therapists can teach you how to make sense of your life, even with the complications. Education in the emotions and in life patterns is a major part of therapy. That is one reason why a therapist would benefit from a big perspective on life, one that does not reduce the soul to the brain or to mere behavior and chemicals. A good therapist is part philosopher and even part theologian, in a nonpartisan way, because the soul touches on the great unsolvable mysteries of life.

Soul Therapy, Not Life Management

What does it mean to focus on the soul rather than on life, and how do you do it?

The soul is a mysterious, deep, and powerful element that infuses all of the self and the whole of life. It is like an immaterial and invisible plasma coursing through every person and the entire universe. It can't be seen on an x-ray, and yet for centuries people have spoken about the soul as a precious power that accounts for their identity and seems to extend beyond the self. Communities, as well as individuals, often use the word *soul*, without defining it, to express how deeply they have been affected by some event—by a tragedy, a death, or a love relationship.

The soul gives you a sense of fate and destiny, even purpose. If you are living a shallow life, unconscious and uneducated, you may just follow the crowd and do what the commercial media tell you to do. You become a consumer whose life goal is more money, more possessions, and a loftier status. You don't understand what human life is all about, and so your life remains shallow. If you are lucky enough to discover the possibility of a soulful existence, you will find meaning and a future. They make all the difference.

Many people, both clients and professionals, think of therapy as adjusting well and contentedly to a shallow culture. But a soul-oriented therapy has a more serious goal. It wants to be close in touch with the source of your existence and to foster a more deeply engaged life. Part of soulful living is being absorbed in life's mysteries: love, illness, marriage, a sense of the eternal and timeless, death and the thought of an afterlife.

When a client comes into my room for psychotherapy, I don't put all my attention on his immediate problems. I talk about what gives him value and what life is asking of him. People, of course, are different from one another. With some I can use the word *soul* and focus on deepening their lives. Others are more concerned with the pressing issue and think of soul as too "religious." So I address the problem but always keep the deep soul in mind. I will discuss one of their dreams that offers some insight into the life problem but also a hint of the mysterious and the timeless. I'll explore one of their life stories that seems to capture the essence of who the person is.

Dreams and the Poetry of a Life

Dreams reveal the deep characters, memories, themes, and fears that are always present though maybe not conscious. And so each time we meet I ask my client for a specific dream with all its imagery. We need access to the depths, and dreams, with all their obscure imagery, reveal patterns and subpersonalities that influence daily life. They show how the past operates in the present by providing images of archetypal patterns and characters, and they are often timely, pinpointing critical matters of the moment.

As a soul-focused therapist, I have to be careful not to get caught up in life issues that are urgent to the client but not deeply relevant. I have to keep at least part of my attention on less visible matters. He says that he's having trouble with a relationship with a woman much older than him. I remember that he's been in this situation before. I remember stories of his childhood and his intense connection to his mother. I recall his habits of eating too much when he's distressed and his tendency to cry when he sees anyone in pain. These factors go together to give me a hint about the man's essence, about his life-defining mythology, or at least one of its main themes, and the person he is behind all the many experiences. I'm getting closer to the immortal, timeless soul. I remember my studies concerning a mother goddess worshipped by men who have unusual sensitivity and feel a strong need to care. I wonder if to this man the older woman is a mother goddess once again appearing in his life.

To see my client's soul I need certain conditions to be present. I need to be calm, not excitable or too adventurous. I can't be blinded by any need to be successful with him or to cure him or to understand his situation completely. I have to listen closely and allow my receptive imagination to be in full power. I keep in mind one of my favorite lines from the poet Rainer Maria Rilke. He describes a flower opening to the morning sun as having "a muscle of infinite receptivity." I try to picture that delicate muscle that opens a flower and find it in myself as I listen to my client's emotion-filled words, which speak at a level even he does not grasp.

The Myth Beneath the Life Story

For the most part, therapy is a matter of telling stories and listening to stories. A therapist needs an acute ear because she has to hear the stories within and behind the stories told and reach so far in her hearing as to grasp the mythic tale, the one that only whispers in the background and yet expresses the essence of the story. Myth describes the basic human experience, the archetypal level, that undergirds the story of events in time. The client tells the stories of her life, but the therapist listens for the rumble of myth deep within the simple stories of life.

Adventures of the soul are bigger in scope than the vignettes of ordinary days. They are captured in myths, fairy tales, and legends, not in personal stories, unless you probe these deeply enough to glimpse the myth. So I always look for the greater story within the simple, literal details of daily life. I listen beneath the surface for the great and ancient tale, the story of the soul. To do this kind of listening, it helps to know mythologies and fairy tales and folk stories.

If I were establishing my own school of psychotherapy, I'd include classes on mythology and folk tales, the stories of the spiritual traditions, and even novels and short stories, all of which educate the imagination so that a therapist is ready to hear the deep rumblings of primal narratives within the telling of a personal experience. A therapist should be an expert in stories, one who not only listens well but also helps clients tell their stories vividly and meaningfully.

Of course, a friend can also detect the great stories hiding with the simple tales from everyday life. Everyone has an opportunity to be educated in the various genres of literature. Even a little acquaintance helps when you are listening to a friend's worries. The great stories often peek through the plain, simple ones.

A friend hearing a tale of depression could say, "You sound like Hamlet. I wonder if he is living in you at this moment."

Classical mythologies involve superhuman figures—gods,

goddesses, nymphs, heroes. Personal mythology consists of events in life that stand out and define a person, including people who were bigger than life and places that have special meaning. Some things that happen in childhood become a constant reference later in life. Certain episodes and personalities have enough weight to act as figures of myth, and certain powerful stories gather together into a personal mythology.

At the cultural level mythology explores the grand themes of existence: good versus evil, loss of consciousness, the quest for soul, the journey aspect of life, life-defining love. Each of us has a parallel mythology that can be told in personal terms: separating from mother and father, competing with a sibling, finding a sexual partner, battling difficulties and obstacles, finding your place in community. These are some of the quests that engage a person's soul.

A man tells me that in childhood his parents favored his brother and gave his sibling many opportunities. My client was seen as the less clever one who did not need an education. He would have an ordinary life without any special opportunities. In fact, the man was quite gifted and eventually successful. But emotionally he still feels neglected and overlooked. Personal success is not enough to overcome childhood memories of neglect.

In a larger sense, the cultural myth in this little story might be the tale of the hero abandoned or left behind. Moses gets placed in a basket and sent down a river, away from his people. The evil witch takes Rapunzel away from her parents and locks her up in a tower all alone. These are powerful tales of abandonment. Maybe they could shed light on this man's feeling of neglect. Maybe his main issue is an early absence of love and attention.

Themes and Patterns

One way to be therapeutic is to pile up stories around a theme. A client's experiences take on layers of images and narrative, and slowly you begin to glimpse a pattern and then a narrative. Your conversations extend and go deeper. Intimacies multiply. Eventually you spot the grand themes of her life.

Therapeutically, it helps to know that our man slighted by his parents is always the boy left alone to make it on his own. This story is now part of his character, indelible and eternal, about someone always looking in vain for special care. The therapist has to be watchful not to enter this drama and unknowingly play the role of a neglectful parent herself, or even the sensitive supportive one. The client might see her in that role in spite of the therapist's intentions to be different. We'll discuss the intricacies of transference later.

The many stories that shape a life often appear in layers, from personal details to larger themes to myths and fairy tales. It helps to know the narrative you are in. Otherwise, all you have are events and emotions. Narrative offers the first layer of meaning and is therefore crucial.

You ask yourself: *What is the underlying plot in my client's story? What is the main emotion? Where is she trying to take me in understanding her? What is her preoccupation?* The questions you ask yourself grow darker. *How does she unconsciously interfere with the therapy? Is she leaving out important parts of the story? What is her bias?*

These questions make your listening suitably complex and sophisticated. A good listener is not just someone who hears everything but someone who hears what is not spoken or what has been suppressed or mangled. The therapist is a detective sometimes, knowing that the client, although wanting to be open and honest, won't tell you the whole story. You don't let this situation make you cynical. You can still love and admire your client. You simply know that human nature is complicated and the deep stories are slow to emerge. Resistance is not usually intentional but rather an expression of the neurosis.

Therapy consists largely of storytelling and storylistening. That is because life is made up of stories. A story has the advantage of often being richly layered, entertaining, provocative, and more revealing than plain facts. So a therapist has to be good at dealing with stories. Stories and dreams: these are the main ingredients of psychotherapy. They give us a clue as to the basic skills a professional therapist should have and the orientation a friend might have after lending an ear and offering help.

Let me summarize by offering a few guidelines with the lay "therapist" in mind:

> Your capacity to be caring and compassionate is your main resource in being with a friend or relative in a "therapeutic" manner.
>
> Look into yourself and distinguish between your needs and those of your friend.

- 14 -

Listen beyond the obvious and literal stories told and hear the bigger, deeper, and more subtle narratives.

You are caring for your friend's soul, not judging or giving advice. Find it in yourself to have an open mind.

Don't think of your friend's life as a problem to be solved but as a complicated experience that she is trying to sort out and do well with. The two of you share that goal in your life as well as hers.

We will add to this list as we get to even more subtle and challenging matters.

A story from life is a
Serious pleasure
Reveals
The hidden, the secret,
And gives dramas
Of the soul
Visibility
The start to psyche's
Therapy.

Chapter 2

THE STORIES WE LIVE

Umberto Eco, the great Italian novelist and intellectual, once wrote: "Every story tells a story that has already been told." If you look closely at any story you tell about your everyday life, you can spot a legend or some other grand tale that has been told for thousands of years. As Joseph Campbell (1949) put it famously, "The latest incarnation of Oedipus, the continued romance of Beauty and the Beast, stand this afternoon on the corner of Forty-Second Street and Fifth Avenue, waiting for the traffic light to change" (p. 4). The great stories of the world are all about our own small daily lives, and the stories about our lives echo the great myths and legends.

Take storytelling out of our lives, and what would be left? Nothing. Everything from a train timetable to a huge dictionary to a scientific laboratory—they are all there as part of larger, greater, and deeper stories. The news of the world comes to us in the form of stories. In a way, all we have are our stories, and so it makes sense that a practice as basic to human life as soul care would be rooted in stories.

Essentially a therapeutic conversation is simple: it is two or more people talking to each other about things that matter. Therapy usually involves one person telling his life stories and the other listening carefully. The therapist speaks but not nearly as much as the client.

Somehow this simple human activity that has been going on since the beginning of time is a "talking cure." There is something profoundly therapeutic in one person listening to the other's stories generously, attentively, and openly. It is one of the primal acts of human interaction, and it has the power to relieve emotional pain and sort out life sufficiently to offer a degree of calm and happiness.

The Levels of a Story

A specialist might say that all stories are multivalent. That means that they operate on several levels at once. The story can be heard in many ways, sometimes even contradictory ways, and the various layers each offer a deep impression. It may be difficult at first to say what the story is about, but it's important to absorb all the layers before arriving at any conclusions. Even your conclusions may be full of contradictions and paradoxes. A good therapist develops what the poet John Keats called "negative capability," "when a man is capable of being in uncertainties, mysteries, doubts, without any irritable reaching after fact and reason."

A patient listener can stay with uncertainty and mystery.

She does not have to explain everything. She can be stupefied by the facts and wonder where to go next. She can be stunned by the complexity of a human life. If she is patient, eventually all that complexity will morph into meaning that calms the emotions.

In therapy, when a person tells a particularly powerful story, you don't have to look for a final interpretation. You enjoy the story, tease out details, and talk about various ideas it offers. Over weeks, months, and sometimes years, that one story may keep coming back for fresh responses. It may keep feeding your evolving understanding of what is going on in this person's life. If you explain the story or interpret it too far, you may kill off this potent source of soul life.

I have learned this lesson slowly over time and from experience. If I can stay open to the story and let it show itself gradually, both the client and I are taken to new places. Sometimes even a resolution will slip out of a story without benefit of clear understanding and with very little interpreting. Over time you can tell the difference between using your mind forcefully to crack open a story and alternately letting its confusing details burst open and present a new approach to the client's life.

Some therapists prefer interpretations and conclusions, but this need for a final resolution can get in the way of taking the story in fully. A story is a living thing. The point is to let it have an impact on you, rather than manipulating it for your own purposes. It may take more presence of mind to receive a story in all its parts than to probe it for a single meaning. You can let the story stir your thoughts and feelings, bringing up memories, ideas, and other stories. You let a network of material spread out from the story, and that web of many details is the meaning. You don't want an easy or concise summary of plot and characters. You want to be moved by the plot and feel acquainted with the characters.

You may think of a life story as stirring the imagination and offering catharsis, a clearing away of confusion and disturbance. A story can enrich your memory and interpretation of events. Many stories, or one story told many times and in many ways, can deepen your reflection on events, giving you a better chance to clear up your emotions about it. You're looking for depth of insight, not the solution to a puzzle.

The professional therapist may have more difficulty with this easy law of stories than the lay therapist. Professionals may automatically think that their job, and the whole point of their education, is to solve mysteries and learn from the stories people tell.

A therapist may personally appreciate certain kinds of stories over others. The client starts talking about a parent or an episode in childhood, and the therapist thinks, *Now we're getting somewhere*. But a story about buying a car that day may be just as revealing.

The amateur is probably less focused on family history and may be more open to all kinds of stories. On the other hand, the nonprofessional may tend to be literal-minded.

The Zen master Shunryu Suzuki (1973, p. 22) said that a Zen student should always have "beginner's mind." "In the beginner's mind there is no thought, 'I have attained something.' All self-centered thoughts limit our vast mind. When we have no thought of achievement, no thought of self, we are true beginners. Then we can really learn something."

The lay therapist helping a friend is probably closer to beginner's mind than the professional, and that is his advantage. From a certain point of view his lack of training is his beginner's mind. Suzuki teaches how to clear your mind of heavy goals and expectations.

Let's not pass over this rich idea too quickly: beginner's mind. It means being unusually open to what a story has to offer, holding back on any need to be clever and solve the story before it has oozed out its real significance. Beginner's mind is not being stupid but rather not being full of prejudice and preconceptions.

Beginner's mind helps me notice my own subtle reactions to a story as it is told. A foreign thought creeps into my head. I could dismiss it, because it has no obvious connection with the conversation, but I don't. I give it a hearing, though I don't know where it might lead. I've come to understand that exploring a person's life narrative is not a logical procedure. You can allow the illogical developments, and often they are the richest ones. These days I often hear myself say, "While you were talking, an odd thought came into my head. Let me tell you about it. I don't know what it means."

A client says, "My father used to drive us kids into the countryside." I hear that simple statement, and a thought comes to me. I ask, "What kind of car do you drive today?" This is not casual curiosity, which is on my list of forbidden responses, but a loose thought, not entirely unrelated, but not logical. The client says, "I drive an Audi. I can tell you I will never own a Ford because that's what my father drove." Then we're off on the subject of her constant anger with her father and her ways of distancing even today. This new theme is not a distraction but an important element that was stuck inside the original story, waiting for detection. A skillful listener uncovers what is concealed in an innocent detail.

A Story's Shadow

Sometimes we romanticize stories. We select positive ones and give them positive interpretations. We think it's always good for clients to tell their stories, and we try to be wide open to receiving them. We expect stories to be uplifting, and it is this positive value that we consider therapeutic. We fail to remember that stories can be misleading, can leave out significant details, and can be rigid.

Stories can have a dark side, too. A person may tell the same story again and again to avoid facing a painful memory or truth. The point of the story may be to hide rather than reveal. The story may cloak unwanted information in a positive narrative covering. You may think that a person is unburdening himself, when in reality he is hiding. The therapist, too, has a dark side insofar as she has to be suspicious, looking for signs that the client is misleading her.

A client does not always tell her stories cleanly and innocently. In telling a certain story or telling a story in a certain way, she may try to help me understand who she is and what she has experienced. She probably understands her life in a certain way and embeds her idea in her story. I can appreciate her intention, but I would rather hear the pure story.

Worse, a client may be trying to keep the conversation in safe territory or protect someone precious to him. Or the way the story is told may be rooted in a deep emotional complex.

Consciously or unconsciously the client is trying to outwit the therapy. He wants it and does not want it. He shows up and then tells a story in a way that might lead the therapist astray.

All these shady aspects of story apply as well to friends trying to sort out a problem. The helper may suspect that he is being led astray and then has to find a way to confront and slowly work around to the more truthful narrative. It would be important for him not to judge his friend for skirting the facts but rather understand that a manipulative story is part of the situation, material for deeper discussion.

A therapist has to be clever. She has to understand that something in people, usually not intended, wants to block the therapy. Therapists sometimes refer to this blockage as *resistance*, but that's an ego word. It might be better to think archetypally. Could it be that the client has a long-standing fear about facing some past event or relationship? Or maybe the client is simply a private person who does not like to say much about herself. Later, we'll consider the myth of Daphne and appreciate that people have an inherent need, which is not neurotic resistance, to protect their privacy and integrity. Their omissions may not be resistance but reluctance.

When you think archetypally rather than personally, the moralism diminishes or goes away. Instead of ego-guilt you see necessity. You don't blame your client for being evasive. Instead, you appreciate that something deep inside the person wants to keep this particular story hidden, and it may be more important to conceal the details than to try to be completely honest.

I often tell clients that I prefer that they don't tell me everything and that they are not completely honest. I don't want to prod them toward overruling their soul's need for privacy. Compliance comes from guilt; while carefully considering what to reveal, and even holding back, is closer to the soul.

People are complicated. Within them are competing urges to get their experience out in the open and to keep it all private. Clients may want to reveal their life and at the same time hide it. All this makes the therapist's main job, listening, more difficult. You have to think and listen polyphonically, appreciating the validity of competing themes and narratives.

The Deceptive Story

Some people are also gullible and preserve the stories that their family members have been telling for years and decades. They haven't considered that the familiar old stories, often entertaining and cherished, are subtle ways to cover up dark family secrets and protect certain beloved family members. As a therapist, I try to keep my Sherlock Holmes skills in play. I'm suspicious about stories that are just too good and noble to be true. Again, I don't literally take a bad view of my client and her family but only recognize human nature at work.

So let's not romanticize stories even as we extol their value. Everything has a shadow, including the stories we tell with apparent innocence. In therapy I always try to consider the opposite of what I'm being told, or at least an alternative version and explanation.

This contrariness is one of the tools I use regularly. I not only consider an opposite position on stories and their interpretations, I usually present my contrary view. My clients are so used to me offering an alternative to their well-reasoned explanations that after they finish telling me what they think, they wait expectantly for me to contradict them. I do this somewhat in a spirit of fun and openness, even though the matter may be deadly serious. I'm not criticizing my clients; I'm playfully giving them my accustomed and often cherished alternative version.

Musical Repetition

I spent many years studying music theory and composition. I find that my musical knowledge helps me in therapy.

One aspect of music that is both subtle and powerful is the way it repeats melodies and harmonies and tiny bits of themes.

Musical repetition often takes place in therapy. A client asks nervously: "Should I tell you that old story again? You must be tired of it." You may ask yourself, *Why is he so anxious about repeating this story?* Then he tells the old story anyway. Rarely is the story exactly as it was the first time. Usually there are variations—a good musical form.

When the story is repeated, you might wonder if the main issue in the story is still unresolved and still bothering your client. Or maybe he needs to be convinced of the validity of the story as he is telling it. He may get pleasure telling you this particular story, and again you have to wonder what that is all about. All this material arises simply because the client repeats a story.

You can invite your clients to tell a story more than once, maybe many times. Give permission for the repetition. People often feel embarrassed telling the same story again and again. Maybe something was omitted in the first telling. Or the next time the story may have certain changes and additions, a different emphasis, or an alternative ending. It is possible that something has been held back, and now it's time to come clean.

On the other hand, the story may simply need repetition so it can be heard and valued better. Repeated tellings in themselves give a story added power and sometimes a bit of ritual. If you hear a story that you've heard before, in addition to new details, you may hear it with greater intensity simply because you've heard it before. Sometimes I'll take the initiative and say, "Would you tell me that story about the boating accident once more?"

As you listen to a story being told, perhaps courageously by a person hesitant to revisit the past, you might hear things they do not hear. You may have a fresh perspective so that, with your ear attuned to the story, it may be told as if for the first time. You may hear nuances not noticed before or may grasp a detail that you had overlooked.

You may say, "What I hear in your story is . . ." Once a woman was telling me how her brother had a habit of hitting her playfully but in a way that hurt. She was complaining, but I said to her: "What I hear in your tone as you tell the story is pride. You sound proud of your brother." At this, she began to cry, because indeed she had mixed feelings. Her story was more about the attention her brother gave her than the aggression in his manner.

Sometimes you may hear something odd in the telling, but at first it is not clear what the issue is. You can point out that word and ask about it. Once a man was telling a story about life at work when he mentioned a window. The word sounded peculiar to me, but I did not know why it stood out. "I know," the man said, "one day my dad dropped some water on me from a window above me. I thought it was mean of him." Off we went, discussing the episode that remained in the man's memory affecting his relationship with his father and all father figures after that.

You might also notice a familiar theme in a personal story. It may be a myth or fairy tale or novel or movie buried in the story that is being told. To see the greater story, the one Umberto Eco talked about, you have to read and study mythology and fiction, which is good preparation for therapeutic listening. It's common, for example, to hear the story of Cinderella when a woman tells how her sisters made her do all the menial work, and her mother liked them more than her. The fairy tale can prepare you to hear and appreciate the story in a bigger way.

Fairy tales give special insight to a life event because they emphasize certain themes like magic, enchantment, struggles with evil, and odd characters that may show up in life. Noticing a fairy-tale theme in a client's or friend's tale may help you notice what the person is trying to say. To sharpen my skills as a listener, for years I have been reflecting on the deeper meaning of fairy tales.

Storyless Therapy

You can't assume that a person is going to have a rich story to tell, or any story for that matter. You need the right emotional conditions to tell an important story. Until those conditions arise, you are in a prestory state. This is just where many clients are. They feel the emotional confusion and pain, but they can't put it into story form. This is a valid condition. It would be presumptuous for a therapist to demand or expect a story before its time. You need patience with the prestory phase, which can last a long time (Estess, 1974).

I don't encourage storytelling when it does not happen naturally. The situation is similar to the feeling of being stuck and not getting anywhere. You allow yourself to be there with what is given. This is a time without stories, even if you theoretically believe that therapy is about storytelling. Everything is defined by its opposite. To be receptive to stories, you have to be receptive to the absence of stories.

Eventually you may arrive at a point where a story can be told. A person may begin with an emotion, some physical discomfort, or some quiet urge to talk or to change. This phase is different from the storyless one. The client sputters and fragments of a story appear. Now you can encourage a story by asking about the emotion or urge. "When did it appear? How does it feel?" A story may come out of this useful curiosity. Often it takes just a hesitant attempt at narrative to transform a mass of feeling into a story.

You can always ask about childhood or the early years. "Did you feel this way then? Did anything happen to bring out feelings like this?" Or simply, "What are your earliest memories?" You'd be surprised how a simple, honest prompt can invite a significant story into the conversation. Then you are in the genre of narrative, where the motor of therapy purrs along.

I say "honest" prompt because sometimes curiosity is shallow, just searching for more information on a lark. Or it is automatic and does not have a purpose. To be of help we need words of power, not of idleness; words that come out of our deep listening and that respond to the subtle tones and revelations we hear. Listening and speaking are the yin and yang of conversational therapy, two sides of a coin, both intense and generous.

I favor an enjoyable conversation as the best model for therapeutic talking, rather than a strained, too focused, and analytical discussion. Not only friendship but friendliness invokes the soul. Remember always that being in the presence of the soul is the main point in psychotherapy, soul care, whether it's done in a therapist's office or between friends at lunch.

> She started to tell her story
> And then stopped,
> Thinking better of it.
> I started listening to her story
> And then stopped,
> Thinking better of it.
> A story has a will of its own
> And knows best when to be told.

Chapter 3

BURIED MYTHS

One of the oddest stories from Greek mythology is the one about the god Hermes. On the first day of his life, as a baby, he notices his brother Apollo's cattle standing in a pasture and wants them for himself. Cleverly he ties small branches to their feet and backs them out of the field so no one will suspect the theft. Then, when his brother complains, he denies that he did anything. "I'm just an infant," he says.

Now this is one of the great gods of the Greeks, adopted by the Romans as Mercury, the patron of language, business, traveling, and the arts. He is the "guide of souls" who links heaven and earth. He is the in-between factor, the connector, highly sexual and phallic, full of shadow, who represents important necessities of life, such as imagination and language skills, but also the darker factors like useful deception, familiarity with the underworld, and comfort with being not so dignified and proper.

I mention Hermes for two reasons: His ways, often on the

margins of propriety, are important for therapy, though they are subtle. Hermes represents the power to use language and images skillfully, to probe multiple levels of meaning, and to value surprise and synchronicity. A Hermes-inspired therapist or helping friend looks for unexpected discoveries and revelations. He is on the sidelines and between the cracks. He spots hardly noticeable remarks and gestures and pays attention to style as well as substance. He has a special eye for shadow qualities, and can sympathize with them, and knows that he can't hide behind his professionalism and satisfied life or the healthy image his clients project onto him.

After just a little experience with therapy, you realize how sharp your ears and mind have to be. A client's passing remarks, so important for understanding her, would be hardly detectable to the average person. It's as though you have several ears, each tuned to a different message being offered. And you have to use language with unusual skill and maneuverability. You need to be clever and witty and own your own shadow qualities.

In league with Hermes, you can move in sync with the other, holding the reins loose enough so that your client can take you to unknown places. You follow so that you can see her world and feel her sensations. You can surrender full control, showing her that it is possible to live with trust, easing up on any anxiety to be in command. One of your tasks is to encourage the soul to come out of hiding.

Life on the margins may mean straying from the customs and requirements of traditional therapy. With Hermes on your shoulder, you may stretch the rules. A client calls to change an appointment and in a friendly way asks how you are doing, and you get into a brief normal conversation. *Should I be doing this? Is it professional? Is there a hidden agenda?* Hermes is nearby, and so you enjoy the brief chat, letting go of your professional paranoia, knowing that a brief friendly exchange of words can serve you both.

The Hermes-type therapist, said Rafael López-Pedraza, one of the founders of archetypal psychology, does not hide in his dignity but gets down into the muck of human struggle and ignorance. A therapist inspired by Hermes is not above his patient, healthy and knowing, but is in touch with his own human frailty. He does not use his rational mind as much as his empathic heart and pays attention to physical details that a more conventional therapist might overlook. He is also sometimes crafty and subtle and not always straightforward.

An online client talking to me on the screen, seeing me in my home setting, says, "I like your office. I always pictured you in a big beautiful house, and in your very sophisticated library." She does not know that I'm actually in a closet of a room, with no space to put things like pens and files and the latest mail. Outside the range of the screen, it's a bit of a mess. But should I take away her illusion? I don't think so. Her image is rich; it does not have to be accurate. I remain quiet. The Hermes in me.

A generous friend listening to another's problem might also avoid the temptation to feel superior. You are not the one with a problem, not now anyway. But remember that you have your own issues and might well consult someone for some therapeutic talk.

I begin this chapter on myth with Hermes because he is

such an important figure for therapy and also to give you an idea of how myth might address issues in psychotherapy. Jung used the Roman name for Hermes: Mercury or Mercurius. But it is essentially the same spirit. He said therapy begins and ends and takes place with Mercurius, the primary mythical figure behind psychotherapy. He works by magic, is always shifting from one level of reference to another, and is colorful.

It's curious that Jung would place emphasis on a figure from myth as the beginning and end of the alchemical, therapeutic process. I have a similar intuition that Hermes is our main inspiration as therapists. And so I begin our discussion of myth with him. But now I'd like to expand our conversation and look at mythology more generally and consider its role in psychotherapy.

A Sensitivity to Myth

Many people today have a positive and intelligent understanding of myth due to the highly effective work of Joseph Campbell, who showed that myth does not mean falsehood or illusion but, quite the opposite, the deepest and most important threads in human experience. Myths are stories about the usually hidden themes that motivate us and reveal the roots of our emotions and passions.

A study of mythology would help a therapist see more deeply into a client's tale of suffering. Myth takes your thinking far beyond personal matters. It describes the grand themes, patterns, and spirits in ordinary life, like Mars's force and aggression, Venus's sensuality and beauty, and Diana's purity and personal integrity. It would be a mistake, though, to think of these figures in such simple, symbolic terms. As we saw in the case of Hermes, they tell of profound, complex, and multifaceted patterns and dynamics in action. These mythic figures are more like actual personalities of the imaginal realm visiting us with their biases and preferences than symbols of human experience (Hillman, 2007).

Another scholar of Greek myth, Karl Kerényi, made a remark in one of his books that helps me understand myth. He was discussing the goddess Artemis and noted that she is the atmosphere you sense when you are deep in nature. Think about going on a hike, moving farther and farther from the civilized world. You sense a pristine purity. That sensation is the essence of the mythic goddess Artemis. You have met her and been close to her. Now when you read about her or imagine her to be at work in you, you know with your senses who she is, and in a way who you are. She is that smell of fresh air, that unspoiled look of nature, and the special feeling of not being in the busy and noisy world or with other people. She is that whole realm of natural purity working through you. She is your natural self, or better, the spirit exuding your natural being.

Artemis is living in you when you need to feel pure and clean, like uncivilized nature. She is there when you want to be an individual and not follow the crowd. She appears when you are angry when people tell you what to do and expect you to be someone else. It is not that Artemis symbolizes your emotions. She is a real presence. She moves you to feel and act in a certain way. You can personify her, feel her to be a personal presence in you and the world, all without being literal about it.

Some authors present myths as categories or templates—boxes with labels in which to put a person's issues. But myth is far more subtle and alive. By studying the great mythologies of the world, you get a bigger and deeper vision of what motivates people and accounts for their choices and actions. You discover that you don't live your life as much as life, in all its variety, lives through you.

We exist in an age of personalism. Psychologically we explain almost all behavior in personal terms. But myth can broaden that view significantly. It personifies factors like Anger, Love, Jealousy, Conflict, Beauty, and this personifying takes these elements out of the objective, too narrowly defined ways in which we usually speak of them. We come to see emotions like anger and love as living forces within us over which we don't have complete power. It's as if they were separate persons acting within us.

Mythology captures the large and powerful forces at work and is universal in scope. A mythological story does not tell just how one person will experience love and loss but how these experiences are common to all people. Mythology presents the archetypal level of experience, that which is common to humanity and at the very roots of experience. A therapist equipped with a knowledge of mythology can better see the basic, human challenges that face us all, here in the unique life of a client or friend.

With a myth-based psychological perspective you may put less blame on the person and instead respect the forces like lust, rage, and justice that are aflame in him. You understand why depression, the malady of Saturn, is so immovable and heavy. Generally you have a greater sense of what it means to be a person. You are not a puny ego but a vast soul that is the home of many powerful forces. This greatly expanded picture of what it means to be a self is one of the strengths of Jungian and archetypal psychology.

With this larger notion of what it means to be a person and a self, let's continue to explore a few specific mythological figures and appreciate how they play their parts in the unfolding of a life.

Persephone

To the Greeks, the myth of Persephone and her mother, Demeter, was one of the major tales of human life. This powerful story lay behind their primary initiation ritual, the Eleusinian Mysteries. In the story, Persephone is a young girl out picking flowers when the ground erupts and Hades, the ruler of the underworld, appears and pulls the girl down into his dark realm to be queen. To appreciate the impact of this tale you have to consider the shattering and profound impact of the transformation from youth delighting in flowers to Mistress of Death. The initiation rite was mainly about facing mortality and finding a way toward hope and happiness.

Myth-minded psychologists have seen this story as one of emotional deepening. We are all sometimes forced into the darkness of despair or the depth of emotion. Women in particular have identified with Persephone, understanding that innocent girlishness needs deepening, often through dark experiences. Many women have told me stories of meeting with rough Hades-like men as a kind of transition out of innocence into real life. Usually the fall into soul is not so dramatic and dark. At these moments dreams may depict a form of descent or destruction that gives more details about the nature of the transformation. Volcanoes, tornadoes, and burning buildings often appear at this point, signaling how deep and comprehensive the developments taking place really are.

I'm reminded of a woman, Sandra, who had an unusual relationship with a highly sophisticated man, Richard. Sandra was married to another interesting man, with whom she felt a brotherly love, but Richard made her feel sexual. With Richard she liked the idea of doing something forbidden, like having a relationship outside her marriage. The sexual relationship was playful and did not involve intercourse. Nevertheless, it was precious to her. Thinking mythologically, I felt that Richard was a Hades figure, whose job was to bring Sandra to a deeper level. I hoped personally that she wouldn't go off with Richard, but as a therapist I was careful not to say anything negative about him. My mythic way of thinking saved me from following through on any judgments I might have made about Richard.

I couldn't imagine working through this complex drama without a mythological reference. Innocent girls, of whatever age, need Hades to come and give them their depth, even if his appearance is dark and dangerous. Richard was always toying with Sandra, luring her into sexual situations, but never being available for a real relationship. For her part, Sandra spent her days selling wedding gowns, an interesting job considering Persephone's marriage to Hades, and getting involved with the latest spiritual craze. Obviously, she needed firmer structure to her thinking and her emotions. She needed Richard in her personal mythic development, but she did not necessarily need Richard the person.

When I taught at the university, I heard more than one dream of a student going to the main library, standing at its elevators, pushing the up button, and then speedily going down. Hearing these dreams, I thought of Persephone being taken into the depths of Hades in spite of her wish to be in the sunlight picking flowers.

I felt that my students may have needed a certain loss of innocence and a downward, deepening experience. They took themselves and life too lightly. For them, partying and romance were the main pleasures and challenges of life. The young men and women both had puella complexes, a young girl's outlook on life, that begged for a matching figure that would be more mature. These students were also being taught through Apollo, with his learning and ideas. But their dreams took them to a very different place, far deeper and darker. At that moment, their "young girl" psyche apparently needed a greater and more shadowy goddess.

I have also had several initiations into a deeper outlook by relating to some women as the young Persephone picking flowers, only to discover painfully that the Mistress of Death was not far away. I have felt deeply betrayed by the appearance of the underworld figure, and as painful as the experience was, it made me less innocent. Persephone offers the gift of maturity.

Remember, too, we are not trying to get rid of the young, flower-loving girl. The innocent Persephone is always present, forever being abducted downward, forever summoning the Queen of Death and Shadow. The myth is complete only when the two sides of the story are in play. You can't have depth without a surface existence, or shadow without innocence. Both the young girl and the Queen of Hell are necessary to the story and the experience.

Many cultures honor a figure like Persephone, like Ala among the Igbo people of Nigeria, a goddess of the fruitful land and of death and the underworld. Or Mictēcacihuātl, the Aztec goddess who with her husband rules the underworld. I focus on Greek mythology only because I know it well and have studied its role in the unfolding of Western culture and in depth psychology.

Daphne

The myth of Daphne is another tale of special relevance to the young. In it a young woman runs away from the attentions of the attractive god Apollo. Sometimes people read this story literally, as if Daphne were a modern woman running away from a rapist or harasser. But myth is not so literal. You see the name Apollo, and you have to consider what he stands for: culture, knowledge, the arts, medicine, music. This is what is trying to capture Daphne's attention, and that could be a good thing. Any young innocent person might do well to study, get involved with the arts, become more culturally sophisticated, and so on.

But there is something Artemis-like (the unmarried goddess of personal integrity and raw nature) about Daphne. It is her nature to be solitary, not identified with a man or with Apollo's highly cultured world. Daphne could be that spirit in us that does not want to be part of a couple or drawn into culture through learning and healing. Any of us might resist more education, even if it would be good for us. We might prefer to live in the organic countryside rather than in the sophisticated city. We want to be free to be ourselves and live in the real world. Henry David Thoreau, choosing to be out canoeing rather than attending a lecture, is quite Daphne-like. Emily Dickinson, too, had a Daphne side, tending the flowers at the family homestead where she lived in nunlike privacy.

Suppose you are counseling a friend who is resisting her parents' wishes that she go to college. Ordinarily you might think that she is just afraid or resistant and might try to convince her to get over her blockages. But if you know the story of Daphne, you may realize that this is not resistance but a part of the young woman's nature, at least at this moment in life, to keep herself intact and not toyed with. Something in her may not want interference from an institution, even if, like Apollo, it has her best interests in mind. Knowing the myth will certainly affect the way you help her. The myth gives you alternatives and saves you from being moralistic in your counseling. You don't have to convince your young friend to leave home and go to school. If she does not want higher education, she may be obeying a necessary impulse in her that the Greeks called "Daphne."

Connecting human challenges to mythological tales has been an important technique for me as a therapist. It helps me see the deep stories being lived out in the obvious narrative of the person in front of me and helps me see the roots of suffering and confusion. I hear the personal story, detect the myth, and, having studied the myth and its meaning, have a fuller picture of what the client is going through.

I don't merely match a behavior with a myth. That's too simple. I prefer to immerse a personal experience or characteristic in a bath of liquid the color of a particular myth. The bath helps me see what otherwise is invisible. The coloring of the myth matches the coloring of the life experience. For example, if a woman tells me she just is not interested in a relationship at this time, I sense the atmosphere her mood creates. It's the atmosphere of Daphne.

Myth and Psychotherapy

I can't overestimate the usefulness of mythology. But some people may not be inclined toward myth. It does not suit their taste. They may be more comfortable with fairy tales, legends, fiction, or poetry. With any form of literature, focus on the details as well as the main plots, and always think metaphor. Don't anthropomorphize the grand figures of myth. Remember, Apollo is not a man; he is the spirit of learning, culture, healing, and music.

Unfortunately, we don't teach our young people how to read stories for relevance. We just teach facts and interpretations and remain on the surface. Incredibly, you may read the story about Persephone and not realize its relevance to your psyche and to some of the challenging experiences you are going through. On the other hand, her tale could be the most important story you have ever read.

Mythology redirects your attention to the deeply human instead of the literally personal. This is an essential move for any therapist, professional or amateur. Your job is not just to help manage everyday life but to see the greater arc of time and the deep narratives that shape every life. Mythology tells the stories that we live at a level far beneath the obvious, and in that way contributes much to a therapeutic way of seeing. These personal myths affect the whole of life, not just a momentary episode.

Sometimes these buried myths are widely known and their presence obvious. Suppose someone were to tell you that one day she arrived late for school and the teacher made her wear a large letter "L" attached to her shirt. It embarrassed her, and now, as an adult, she feels shame whenever she arrives late for an event. You could refer to Hawthorne's *The Scarlet Letter* because of a similar theme, except that in Hawthorne the letter "A" for *adulteress* was more serious. Still, the literary story, which comes close to the stature of a myth, might help you appreciate aspects of the personal story. You have to allow for differences of detail.

Looking for the buried myth is a major technique in the psychology of C. G. Jung, who began to develop his theories at the time of Freud. He spoke of "amplification" as a method of looking more deeply into the imagery of dreams and stories. You amplify by comparing the dream image, say, to a known myth. The idea is that mythology tells the stories that portray the universal themes in all human lives: love, struggle, anger, death, illness, family. If you study the myths and learn the subtleties of human experience, then you may be less moralistic about what is going on. You see necessity, as I mentioned before, instead of right and wrong. If you are acquainted with the myth or have studied it, you will address your client's story with that knowledge in your tool bag.

The study of myth would be a good preparation for a therapist who wants to go deep with a client, and perhaps behold Exodus playing out, the liberation from some bondage he is in, or the Odyssey in an ordinary person's life—a journey back to where she feels at home and belongs.

Through his knowledge of mythology Jung was able to see meaning in the apparent gibberish of people being treated in a psychiatric hospital. He (1973) said that a story is more important than a diagnosis: "Clinical diagnoses are important, since they give the doctor a certain orientation, but they do not help the patient. The crucial thing is the story. For it alone shows the human background and the human suffering, and only at that point can the doctor's therapy begin to operate" (p. 124).

Diagnosis can take away the individuality and complexity of a client's experience. It puts a client into a box. It serves the therapist more than the client. It can be demeaning. It places the therapist above the client. A diagnosis can be full of shadow, even if it might please the client to have a name for what he's going through. That, too, is an illusion. Now we know how to treat the syndrome, and we don't have to face it as a unique invitation to become an individual. The diagnosis puts you in a pen with other people who have given up their individuality, as well.

Your story is individual. Remember Hillman's warning to keep your images, your stories, exactly as they present themselves. Don't adjust them so they fit into a box of syndromes and disorders. Each time you tell a story it is different—different nuances and tones. You call up a story from the past and you tell it in the present with the full impetus of who you are right now.

Myth, so outrageous
It can't be literal.
Forces you deeper
Than you thought possible.
Suddenly a glimpse
Of what is going on
And what to do.

Chapter 4

THE SYMPTOM AS A VEHICLE OF CHANGE

A ground rule in archetypal psychology: "Go with the symptom." I watched James Hillman use it constantly, and Patricia Berry has written about it, providing good theory to support the practice. Acting out a complex can sometimes lead to the discovery of a vibrant and centered self—when it is discussed and reflected upon in some form of deep therapy.

Berry's (1982) idea is simple: a symptom does two things at once—it defends us against any change that is needed, and it shows the way forward (pp. 81–95). It gives an indication of what is needed and perhaps trying, in an awkward way, to be noticed. A client says that she is always being controlled and manipulated by other people. She is never forceful or independent enough. In fact, she easily becomes dependent on almost anyone she has to live or work with. She often feels defeated and humiliated, and she comes to therapy hoping to become stronger.

This is a painful situation that many could identify with. If you were this person's friend, and she asked for your help, you would likely try to pump her up and help her to feel good about herself and find her strength. But you would be taking her words at face value, and they could easily be manipulating you. She may be confused about what is going on and fail to notice tendencies within herself to control people and situations because they represent an unconscious opposite to qualities with which she identifies. Often a person who is obviously weak and pushed around is actually quite forceful in ways that are not obvious.

She wants to be stronger, but the symptom, if you regard it with some sympathy, points toward being weaker, perhaps vulnerable. I would follow our principle and listen closely to what the symptom wants. Where is it headed? The symptom itself does not point toward being stronger. Therefore, I wouldn't become the cheerleader for power. Here is someone who needs to learn better how to let others have some power and influence over her without her feeling too dependent.

I understand how counterintuitive this position is. Most people might think it obvious that what is needed here is independence. But just beneath the surface you might notice a tendency to be in control. You see the dependency clearly, but you may also glimpse her subtle and probably unconscious ways of taking charge. She feels the passivity sharply but does not notice her controlling habits. An added problem is that the unconscious power she wields may be excessive and ineffective because it is not up-front. Being strong is not yet part of her personality, and so it is an autonomous, compensating complex, a stray behavior that comes out of her without any consciousness and purpose.

A therapist has the advantage of experience with the client and may recognize the symptom and how it fails her. You may already know that this is someone who does not listen well, always wants her own way, and gets people to do her will without being honest about it. Seeing the contradiction, you are in a good position to address it.

This common pattern may be so hidden to a therapist that he gets pulled into sympathy for the defenseless woman. But things are not as they appear to be, and you need a trained, sometimes suspicious eye to catch the inverted nature of this symptom. The general principle is: strong complexes almost always come in two extreme parts, one clear and visible and the other fuzzy and hidden.

Power issues play out in all human interactions, and illusions are common. The strong look weak, and the weak look strong. My suggestion is: be guided by the symptom. Sometimes a person will be what we call a "control freak." This is a different symptom, and in this case we help the client become more powerful. If the symptom is dependency, we help the person become effectively vulnerable.

I find that by approaching a symptom in this way, it morphs over time into a much better version of itself, and language for it shifts. The symptom of being too dependent becomes the virtue of being appropriately vulnerable and open to influence. Anger becomes personal power. Jealousy becomes a capacity for intimacy and interdependency.

A Divided Soul

Here's another rule: when an aspect of character gets split in two, like personal power divided into passivity and control, then we aim for a condition in which both elements are present and influencing each other. Vulnerability keeps power within limits and expressed more gracefully. Power makes vulnerability stronger, less likely to devolve into passivity.

In this way, the therapy has been subtle. The therapist has not gotten caught in the client's strong point of view but has stepped outside of it. The therapist is seeing the situation differently, and that itself may be helpful. When therapist and client are not in the same narrative, there is space for change. Hillman (1983) once defined countertransference— the therapist getting caught in the client's complex—as a therapist indulging in the client's narrative (p. 16). Neutrality means steering clear of a client's contagious and beguiling symptom.

Sometimes I will do nonsensical things to keep from being locked in with my client's drama of opposites. I'll move on to another topic. I may ask at that moment for a dream. I may reach toward my bookcase for a relevant poem. These are signifying gestures, meant not only to get out of a manipulative or sterile direction but also to be mildly dramatic to make a point about what is happening at the moment. I can't be pulled into my client's complex, and I have to be in charge for a moment. I could be teaching her how not to get caught in a stray spider's web of emotion.

Still, I want to stay close to the symptom, the complaint, and not be lured into its opposite. The client, of course, thinks that the opposite place is glorious, the solution, happiness. The woman who thinks she is too weak would like desperately to be strong and powerful. But in fact she is already forceful, only her power is not effective and is hidden to her eyes. She does not know she is so controlling and full of muscle in her relationships. But if you were to talk to her friends, you would probably hear many stories about her annoying power issues and tendency to control. People who identify as being passive are often hyperactive and strong-willed.

You can explore stories, especially childhood ones, when she felt overpowered and not able to get her way. But you can also discuss her fear of giving in and being influenced. The early stories, remember, don't have to be heard as literal history but as narratives at work in her life today. Going back is really going deep.

The client believes she has become too dependent and needs to get strong. But her belief is symptomatic, a complaint, keeping her from being truly dependent in an effective way. Her symptom protects her from moving in a direction that would be good for her. Vulnerability is the last thing this client wants to experience. Yet the symptom also shows that is the very direction we need to go. So, instead of exploring many ways to be strong, we consider ways she might be open to someone else's ideas and direction.

An informal therapist also has to watch out for the drama of opposites. You can be sure that your friend will want you on her side, agreeing that she has been pushed around by others and hasn't felt her own power. She will say that she needs to be stronger and wants your help. This is where it gets interesting in therapy. Your friend, to whom you are devoted, wants you to go in a direction that you can see is not good for her.

You might notice the pattern at work and not get pulled into her view of things. Sometimes there are signs that help you. Your friend may be too obviously manipulative or overly passionate about her position. You may feel that you are being coerced to respond in a certain way, a signal that it's time to go further toward the symptom. Rather than do what she says, you need your own clarity of vision and personal strength. It's interesting how in this example the helper has to deal with a similar pattern: Can he remain strong when his friend's complex wants him to be compliant?

Strong emotions may be contagious. Remain neutral. Be patient as your friend realizes that you aren't going to join her in her wishes. But even as you detach from all the fireworks, remain loyal and available. You can do these two things at once. You are helping her by not doing what she wants you to do. You are refusing to mirror her complex, which might be a pattern of control and gullibility.

Remain Cool When the Therapy Heats Up

C. G. Jung used images from alchemy to guide him in exploring the psyche, one of which is temperature. The alchemist used an oven to heat his materials, and the therapist today tends the emotional temperature through actions like confrontation (heat) and backing away (cool). Although I do turn up the heat intentionally at times, generally I try to remain cool.

Conscious of emotional temperature, I also keep in mind a moment from the classic tale of Eros and Psyche. Psyche is a young girl going through various trials on her path to maturity when she finds herself in the underworld river Styx. She has been instructed not to respond when people there beg for her help, and, sure enough, hands and arms rise up out of the water as men and women entreat Psyche to help them get out of their dire situation. Psyche has to remain unaffected. She can't show them any warmth or her initiation will fail. Remaining cool is a test of her dedication to the process.

I often think of this episode in the tale when my heart is breaking, hearing a sad story of separation or failure. I try to stay *cool*, another word for *neutral*.

The Chinese *Tao Te Ching* teaches a paradoxical blend of soft and hard. "Yield and overcome," it says. It adds, "An ignorant person is always doing something, and yet much is left undone."

Notice the complexities in dealing with clients, who may confuse you with their indirection, which is usually not intended but part of their general lack of psychological sophistication. Unless I'm dealing with a very anxious person, I will usually educate him on this point about following the lead of the symptom. Usually people get the idea quickly and can use it themselves.

Because symptoms point the way, they are valuable. You

don't want to get rid of them at any cost. You see through them to their ultimate value and wisdom. You may even have to reconcile to the fact that the symptoms will diminish and yet remain for later work on them. That's all right. You don't have to eliminate them, but only watch them weaken as you adopt their hidden positive values. You want to see the symptoms fulfilled, not eradicated.

We all have complexes, areas of life where we are too emotional and blind. We act from these complexes, and they are the bulk of our symptoms. If you want to help someone with these habits, you have to be clever enough not to get caught yourself. You have to be somewhat contrary and willing to steer away from certain neurotic expectations of the client. This response may not please the client, but you can make clear to the client what is going on. You may be explicit about your determination to care for the person's soul, assuring him of your devotion in spite of his disappointments.

A symptom is an odd thing,
A pain in the butt
That can give you the best
Idea of what to do next.
But to see it for what it is
You need bifocals or polyfocals.
It has layers and parts
And likes to hide in the shadows.

Chapter 5

BEWARE THE TRANSFERENCE

Whenever you interact with people, more is happening beneath the surface of awareness than you know. You can discover this hidden region of activity if you explore interactions after they have happened. Eventually you may find that old events, sometimes going way back into childhood, are often playing out. There is a *transference* from a past event to the present, and the psyche may *transfer* emotions and meanings from one situation to another, from one key person in the past to someone in the present.

You don't usually make these connections consciously. They happen beneath the threshold of your awareness and affect both the interaction and the relationship. The psyche is always active, even when you sleep, and has its own goals and purposes that are not easy to understand, at least until they have played out. These underlying activities affect your behavior and may confuse you and interfere with your life. It helps to glimpse them and reflect on them so you know more about the dramas taking place in the underworld of your daily experience.

According to Jung, transference is not the literal behavior of the parents and child playing a role later in life, but the archetypal and unconscious complexes in those early relationships. Hillman went further, saying that the psyche is always moving images around from one occasion to the next. The pattern experienced in childhood never goes away but keeps appearing throughout life. It is not just childhood fantasies that get transferred, and not just early ones, but any remarkable images that were present in the past may find a role in current situations. You may use the name of your former spouse when speaking to your current partner, an embarrassing slip that indicates how present a transference may be.

We warn our friends not to get married "on the rebound." The fear is that the images that are so fresh from the previous relationship need time to fade. Otherwise they may interfere with a new relationship. The psyche may transfer them vividly from the past to the present. We not only make slips of the tongue but may engage in more serious transfers of a former relationship to the present one.

It's an ancient idea that people we get close to become part of us or have a room in the hotel of our psyche. We may need to clear it all out sometimes to be able to start afresh. Personally, I want to put some distance between me and James Hillman in my writing and my practice. His imagination was so strong that it affected me deeply. On the whole, I am grateful for it. I can often feel his spirit in me in a positive way, but it can also be too much. He gets transferred into my own identity and work, to the point that sometimes I can't remember where he stops and I start.

Marsilio Ficino (1975) said that your friends eventually live inside you and so do your teachers. In a letter to his friend Giuliano de' Medici he wrote: "My great love for you has long impressed your image on my soul. And just as I sometimes see myself outside myself in a mirror, so very often I see you within me in my heart" (p. 108).

Then when you encounter someone in the present, one or other of these inner figures might come to life and insert themselves. You may actually sense their presence: you may move your body like someone you knew or have their inflections in your voice. Your emotional reaction especially may remind you of someone or a relationship you once had.

The figure from the past is present, but that figure is not the actual person. You are dealing with an imaginal figure who, like someone you know in a dream, is not entirely like the person from life. Imaginal figures have their own qualities as well as some borrowed from the actual person. The person transferred is not just a memory but also an archetypal, maybe even a mythic presence.

For instance, you may go to a bank manager and find that he reminds you of an old friend who happened to be a father figure to you, a difficult one at that. You may well experience similar difficulties with the manager. Your issue then is the archetypal father conveyed through the image of an old friend.

Even though transference does not require a parent figure, mother and father have special places among images that come up in transference. The power of the parents is so great that you never get over their influence. Nevertheless, you should not automatically think of every transference as involving a parent. The psyche may just as easily transfer a teacher, a lover, or an authority figure who can complicate your relationships.

Occasionally in therapy I discover that it is not the parents who have the main role in a person's life and transferences but a grandparent or an uncle or aunt. Certain people make a deep impression on us, and they linger in the psyche and sometimes play a role in later life.

Read the following passage from Jung's book on the transference closely. He (1966) described it as "brought about by the projection of archaic infantile fantasies which were originally vested in members of the patient's own family" (p. 217). Notice that it is not the shifting of family members to a current person, but rather archaic fantasies that were once focused on the family are now wakened in present circumstances. Transference is rooted in the tendency of the psyche to produce images and narratives at all times. It is especially active in the intimacy of a therapeutic encounter.

Contagious Ghosts

I mentioned before that emotions can be contagious. If you are the helper and there is a transference from the past onto you, you are in danger of getting caught up in it and playing your role unconsciously in that narrative—countertransference. You may find yourself in the middle of a highly emotional drama and not aware of what is taking place. You don't realize that your client has found a doctor or an uncle in you.

I remember a client telling me that I reminded her of a former boyfriend who, like me, was interested in art and music and spirituality. That's all it took for a transference to form. If I had unconsciously felt her interest in me through her old boyfriend, I might have developed a countertransference, an added layer of interest due to the eros flowing between us. That could be a useful complication, but it could also cause trouble. In this case I kept my wits about me and cautiously used the frisson of the boyfriend to keep the therapy warm and deep.

A therapist always needs a seat in the back row, where she can watch the drama as it unfolds. She should have the skill to observe several levels playing out at once. At the same time, she has to play her part in the action. She has to be involved with a heightened level of awareness.

It is particularly dangerous to get caught in a transference/countertransference because you may intensify the narrative that is causing the person so much pain, and, of course, in that state you can hardly find your way out to clarity and freedom. It's an illusion for a therapist to believe that he is beyond getting caught up in unconscious activity or that he can get out of it easily.

This is where Jung's warning is especially apropos: you, the therapist, have to deal with your own inner figures as much as your client does. Don't demand everything from your client and absolve yourself from the therapeutic process. You have to face your countertransference, your own participation in the client's hidden theatrics, and work it through. Countertransference means that you are not outside the emotional fantasies flying around in the therapy. You are also a participant.

Early psychoanalysts felt that transference is a way toward healing. You, the conscious one, can show a person how to handle the situation better. Transference becomes an educational opportunity. But that kind of thinking may underestimate the emotional power of the transference and the confusion it can cause. Jung once said that transference could be helpful, but it is so full of illusions and potentially painful, it would be better to avoid it.

What if your client or friend falls in love with you, "transferring" her feelings about her father or dead husband, say, to you. What a mess that could be. What if a man transfers to you, a woman, feelings he had toward an old girlfriend? It's not easy to navigate such a charged situation. You may easily misinterpret what is going on, and your client or friend might misunderstand your intentions. You may both misread the signals and end up in an emotional tangle.

I feel that I have a transference with every client. Everyone stirs up reactions in me that are related to someone else. Umberto Eco said that every story has been told before. I would say that every person I meet I have met before. Much more is going on in every encounter than what appears to be factual and evident. The psyche is always at work behind the scenes.

If you are strong and self-aware, you may like the challenge of a transference, but even then you should probably notice your confidence and bravado. It could be a sign of your unconsciousness. Sometimes you have no choice. You slip into your client's inner drama and then have to be especially insightful and emotionally strong. It makes sense that working out this mess may be educational for both you and your client, and it could help you with the material of the therapy. The mutual transferences are like a new batch of raw material.

Not every emotional situation is a matter of transference. You may feel some strong emotions that simply arise from conditions. But often, maybe even most of the time, you can track intense feelings back to an earlier encounter. You may think of the past as past, but it is also always present and ready to complicate whatever is going on now. You could assume that past experiences are always in the wings, able to show themselves quietly at the slightest provocation.

You should know that the psyche is at work continuously and feverishly, producing emotion-filled images by the minute. Usually they are subtle, purposeful, and complicated. Obviously, if you can ferret out a past model, you have material for soul work. You can talk about the earlier contact with reference to what is going on in the present. It could be rich material for the alchemy of therapy. But you have to be alert lest you simplify in your mind what is actually a very complicated layering of narratives.

You can relate differently, as your own person, more conscious, one hopes, than the person from the past, and maneuver toward a much better outcome. Your client may find some clarity in that. But, as I said, these are dangerous waters, and you may find it difficult to remain clear yourself. On the other hand, you have little choice since transference means an active imagination, and it is at work constantly. It might be better to be open and up-front about the whole process.

Irvin Yalom (2003) gave a relevant example from his own practice, gently inviting work with transferences: he said to his patient, "Perhaps I can help you understand what goes wrong with relationships in your life by examining our relationship as it is occurring. . . . If I can make observations about you that might throw light on what happens between you and others, I'd like to point them out. Is that okay?" (p. 115).

Yalom articulated the part of transference that connects other relationships with the relationship to the therapist. But we might keep Jung's idea in mind that it's not as simple as all that. It is the psyche, the living day-to-day imagination, that causes you to remember unconsciously, if I may say that, a deep archetypal encounter from the past that has come to life again in the present. Your parents are not entirely to blame for the mother or father images that come to life now. They are not the originators but rather an early instance of the appearance of the parental myth.

The Jungian addition makes a difference in therapy. It takes the transference out of the purely personal realm and places it in the region of myth. You can talk about events that took place at home with parents and siblings, but you always remember that these stories have a deeper, archetypal background that better portrays what is going on in the present.

Let me give you an example from my practice. Once, a friendly and kind man came to me professionally to help him get a divorce and marry the woman he loved. From the first moment I felt at ease with him and enjoyed his company. This reaction should have been a clue to me of some kind of transference—transference is happening all the time and can be so subtle that you don't see it. To this point, all I mean is that he and I were in a drama that I felt more intensely than usual.

I sat back comfortably and tried to help. Our conversations were intense, and the dream work we did was helpful. Week after week, slowly he seemed to be gathering courage to make a break with his wife. He had young children and felt so protective of them that he couldn't imagine hurting them with his decision to move on.

Let me give him a name, Howard. As I look back now on that episode, I imagine that my countertransference, my collusion in his story, was to Howard. I had many qualities of character, good and bad, in common with him.

The therapy went quite well, and eventually Howard made his move and ended up in a good place. He even worked through some central aspects of character so that by the end of our work he was a stronger, more decisive and effective man. But looking back, I can now see how my own material got mixed in with his—transference.

When I tell this story now, I wonder how I managed to help Howard. But it seems that my ability to identify with him helped me have great empathy for his situation and perhaps better understanding. On the whole, I don't think that my countertransference seriously interfered. But, as Jung would say, I was fortunate.

Transferring Archetypes

Sometimes the archetypal aspects of a transference are clear. Suppose a young woman were to come to me for therapy, and I quickly imagined her to be a daughter. Again, a first glance that takes in so much of physical presence, character, and emotion is all that is needed to establish a transference that can last for years. I may relate to this woman from that moment on as a daughter, my own fatherly feelings dominant and probably interfering at times. Another aspect of the transference: once established, it may never fully go away.

In this case I may or may not be transferring the reality of my own daughter. It could be just the image of Daughter suddenly coming alive. Because it is a transference, archetypal in this case—daughter as Daughter, not just my own daughter—it is very likely that I will overdo my response to her in some ways. The transference could create a mess, as the daughter archetype has done for me in the past, or it might allow for a strong psychological connection that will help the therapy. Often both occur: you can have a powerful transference without disastrous confusion.

I find that the best way to prepare for inevitable transferences, those powerful and yet unsuspected images from the psyche, is to always be alert to what is going on in your fantasy life. Expect figures to emerge. Don't let them go by unnoticed. Talk about them. Get to know their trends and patterns. This is a soul-oriented way of self-knowledge. Not intellectual knowing, but imaginal knowing.

Being up-to-date with your dreams can help, knowing current trends there and strong images of the moment. If a transference develops, you may notice it in your dreams, not explicitly, of course, but in disguise. You may dream of an old flame, a very common dream theme.

The arrival of strong, somewhat unrealistic feelings for

someone you are guiding keeps you closely connected as the therapy progresses. Let me give another example from my experience. I met Terry at a conference. I admit that my first response was a reaction to her physical beauty. I noticed, if only for a moment, how striking she looked, both her face and figure. But it was a passing glance.

Later, after the conference was over, she phoned and asked if she could do some therapy with me. We got into some of the most intense therapeutic work I have done, and it went on for years. In the end she got through some very difficult emotions based on childhood experiences and arrived at a point where she was free of some of the most painful material. On the other hand, she was poised at that point to begin a new phase. We parted then, but I felt that the next challenges in her life would be part two of an intense period of caring for her soul.

My point is that a minor Venusian archetypal transference set it all off for me at that first meeting. It quickly receded, but I felt that Venus's initial blessing, a slight attraction, helped me stay involved when things got difficult and also, as a faint background hue or hum, sustained the long and challenging work. This, too, was an archetypal transference, a mythical goddess and not a parent, but unique in that it had no personal echo, as far as I can see, and it did not offer any problems, as it might well have done. The difference may have been that I recognized the transference as such, it was not at all overwhelming, and I saw from the beginning how it could help keep us focused.

It's difficult to imagine any human interaction that does not involve transference of some kind and degree. It helps to know the dynamics of the transference in general and to be aware of the exact nature of the transference in play in every therapeutic relationship. The emotion can be one of many: love, hate, envy, pity, brotherly, daughterly, pure care. It helps to be aware of how the transference assists you and how it could get in the way.

Let me go a step further. I suggest that, especially as someone interested in therapy at some level, you assume that every human interaction involves a transference of images and emotions of love, power, fear, or some other basic human feeling. Imagination is in play everywhere and at all times. The air is full of people from the past and elsewhere, and they are always getting involved in your life. You are always in narratives, and one myth or other is always rumbling in the depths of your encounters. Listen to them and know something about the stories and characters that are living through you and between you and others.

In general, a therapeutic attitude asks for a high degree of self-awareness and the capacity to admit to embarrassing vulnerabilities—thus, my personal stories in this chapter. It's embarrassing enough to be out of control, to have highly emotional developments when you're trying hard to be either professional or generous.

So don't just do therapy. Be a therapist. At all times. Always see through to deeper narratives. Listen with your sharpened ear. You are training yourself to "see through," in Hillman's language, to expressions of soul, by means of images, in all interactions. If you are a therapist in your very being, you won't have to rev up your skills when faced with a challenging client or a needy friend.

If you are a lay therapist, a friend helping a friend, you may never have heard of transference or find the idea mystifying. You don't have to use the term, but you do have to be ready for unexpected strong emotions, in your friend and in yourself, that affect the relationship. If you want to be a good helping friend, you might take the time to study transference and how to deal with it.

A transference sounds like a mechanism
You can diagram and work like a machine.
But it's really like loving something so much
That you keep finding it year after year
In various disguises.
Remembering helps,
If you can spot the resemblance.

Chapter 6

SERENITY

The word *serene* originally referred to a clear sky and comes from the Greek *xeros*, "dry." When you are serene, you don't let storm clouds arrive and disturb your peace. One of the best examples of serenity I know is a classic Zen story: A shaken family brings their daughter to a monk and tells him she just gave birth and he, the monk, is the father. He responds: "Is that so?" He takes the baby and cares for it. Years later the family comes again and says, "You are not the father," and the monk says, "Is that so?" He gives the child back to the family.

I know from my many years in Catholic monastic life that monks look for serenity and achieve it to a considerable degree in their community life. Therapists could do the same, since their work requires, at least at times, a cloud-free day so they can be with their clients without reacting unconsciously. Could you reach the level of serenity in that Zen monk? Maybe the extreme example will inspire you, as it does me.

Serenity is not the suppression of conflict or emotion but the achievement of calm through a big enough vision of life that troubles don't take it away, especially in those moments when you need it. Know the difference between the inclination to react unconsciously and the ability to maintain a greater vision that is ready to go into action in a split second.

Another word for professional serenity would be *neutrality*. You have prepared yourself not to become excited at unexpected provocations. You have learned how to be calm though not uninvolved. You remain serene and neutral. Using our weather imagery, the Greek philosopher Herakleitos said, "Like a ray of sunshine, the most enlightened and developed soul is dry." This probably means not wet with the wide-ranging emotions and acting-out of ordinary life. By the way, Herakleitos uses our very word *xeros* for "dry."

It's difficult not to get caught in the emotions that come up in almost all attempts to help people navigate their lives. The best way I know not to get caught is to be neutral from the very first instant. Remember how quickly transferences take form. You meet the Devil or Shadow in a slick salesman. You meet the Lover in a woman dressed just so. You meet the Mother in any caring person, even a young woman just giving you directions. The moment you feel a slight wave of enchantment, go neutral. Remember who you are, a therapist and not an ordinary person. You are not allowed to be unconscious. And you could be like this, serene, all day long and every day because you are a therapist, not just someone who practices therapy. Or you are a friend who at this particular time is an accidental therapist, doing informal therapy for a fellow human being.

The Devil, the Shadow, and the Lover are deep personalities that color the actual person you are caring for. It's possible to be so swayed, charmed, or turned off by these figures that you can't see the real person. You are in myth, and the people you are engaged with are mythic, at least characters in a fiction or drama. Of course, if you carry this idea to its limit, then there is no one at any time that you connect with who is not a figure of myth. You are always in imagination, never contacting anyone or any place free of the narratives that underlie your perceptions. But in spite of all the static, you want to do your job and live a responsible life.

All this complexity and all the signifying layers don't have to be a problem. They account for life's richness. The trouble is, we are usually under the illusion that the world we encounter is a factual one having only one layer we call reality. If you follow the archetypal, essentially Platonic view, there is no reality, absolutely none, that is not colored every day by the living imagination. The therapist does not have the luxury to live and work under the illusion things are as they appear to be. She has no choice but to deal with the imaginal realm, with its unending flow of stories, images, and personalities.

Mundus Imaginalis

This world of imagination often goes by its Latin name, *mundus imaginalis*. *Mundus* means "world," as in "mundane." *Imaginalis* is obvious, but we have to distinguish "imaginal" from "imaginary." The imaginal realm is not imaginary, unreal, but rather that level of perception where images are prominent and have their own reality. We take them seriously, not as symbols for something in the factual world but as real presences.

A few odd examples might help make this point. Kids believe in Santa Claus as a physical being like any other person though blessed with special powers. Many adults sense the spirit of Christmas, but they no longer "believe in" Santa Claus. Many people enjoy visiting 221B Baker Street in London to see how Sherlock Holmes lived. They want to see his pipe and hat and "rooms." They know he is a fictional figure, but they can still picture him as historical. Santa and Sherlock are imaginal figures.

Figures of the soul are not always so "real." They can help us with the work of our everyday lives, as Muses, Artists, and Inspirers. We like to rationalize them as qualities: talents and skills. But they come to us as imaginal persons. The Public Speaker in me has a biography and changes over time. He matures. He is not just a role I play but a person of a certain kind who does things that I alone can't do.

The Public Speaker is not a part of me or an aspect of myself. To put it that way is too rational. The Public Speaker is another person who lives in the imaginal realm. I can call on him to do a job for me, but strictly speaking he is not me. This kind of separation between the figures of the psyche and me helps keep everything clear and helps me not to interfere. I have more power in my life when I can let these figures do their job. As Hillman said, we should speak of "they," not "we."

One way not to get caught in your client's whirlwind of fantasy is to acknowledge the presence and autonomy of the imaginal figures. In my previous example of Venus getting hold of me with a client, I was able to navigate it by sensing Venus's presence. She *seemed* present, and I felt her doing her work. Knowing that she was present allowed me to take the appearance of my client as having a mythic dimension. Venus had actually shown up. But remember, she is never a factual presence, only an imaginal one. At the same time, I know that imaginal figures have more power than purely factual ones.

The Greeks understood how an imaginal figure can dwell in a human being. In the long *Homeric Hymn to Aphrodite*, the goddess is attracted to a young shepherd and disguises herself as a human girl. He sees the girl and only suspects that a goddess might be present. "She did not want him to recognize her and be afraid." He has his suspicions but connects with her anyway.

I try to relate directly to figures of imagination, never seeing them merely as symbols for something in the "real" world. Some Jungian psychologists recommend direct conversations with the figures or drawing them and painting them as Jung did in his *Red Book* (the large illuminated volume of images and mysterious writings). I prefer simply to relate to them in everyday settings, like figures standing next to people. I behold them, notice their influence on the events around me, and take them seriously into account. I don't want to anthropomorphize them.

Neutrality

I recommend that you remain neutral. "Neutrality and patience" is my mantra. Don't lose your equilibrium in some powerful attraction or repulsion. Don't be too available or too remote. Don't be either defended or eager. Use neutral language and gestures. Don't defend against temptation, just don't be available to it.

A potential client says to me, "I've read your books. They've saved my life. It's a dream to have an opportunity to have your personal guidance." I hear this kind of sentiment once in a while. I suppose I should be enthusiastic and honored. Instead, I keep calm, I decline the opportunity to be flattered. I don't need praise now, in this situation, for my work and accomplishments. I'll get that elsewhere. Here we both need neutrality and calm. So, as honestly as I can, I simply say, "Okay, let's see if this works for us. Time will tell."

Frequently I have therapists as clients, usually for a combination of therapy and supervision. Sometimes I sense the awe they feel in the presence of an admired author, so I say, "Let's be colleagues."

There are moments in almost every session of therapy when my chosen action is to not speak. When I hear flattery, I don't respond. Of course, it's good to accept a compliment with grace, but it's also good to be neutral. When I get criticism, I try to remain neutral. If someone expresses immense gratitude, I say, "You're welcome." As I scan the possible responses in my mind, maybe none of them is without its dangers. So I don't speak, or I use a conventional phrase for its neutrality.

When I say, "Time will tell," I mean the gods, fate, and universal will. I am not the center of attention here. I know that anything that is accomplished will be the work of the gods and goddesses and angels, all of whom I trust and believe in. The British poet William Blake said that he was not the author but only the secretary. The authors are in eternity. Similarly, as a therapist I am only the hired hand doing the work of the gods. All that talk about me saving people's lives is kind and well-intentioned, but I should never be tempted to believe it. When people tell me, as they will no doubt tell you, that therapy saved them, I take it as an opportunity to practice neutrality.

If you are not to get caught in your client's or friend's fantasies and words of praise, you have to know fully ahead of time that you are the servant and secretary, not the one who heals and saves. You are the priest and minister but not the cause of success. Your job is to assist at the healing but not do the work firsthand. Sometimes I think of my job as that of a sacristan. I keep the temple clean and well supplied.

If you can cultivate this kind of gentle neutrality in the face of the gods, you have a better chance of not getting caught. There is a natural tendency to adopt the rush of emotion for yourself. You may feel bigger and better because the weather around transference has brushed against you. Again, Jung strongly advised against being contaminated by the figures of the *mundus imaginalis* (he used the term "unconscious").

In his memoirs Jung (1973) wrote: "To the extent that I managed to translate the emotions into images—that is to say, to find the images which were concealed in the emotions—I was inwardly calmed and reassured. Had I left those images hidden in the emotions, I might have been torn to pieces by them. . . . I learned how helpful it can be, from the therapeutic point of view, to find the particular images which lie behind emotions" (p. 177).

We see here that Jung felt strongly that he needed the particular images that could contain certain emotions; otherwise, he'd be torn apart. We'll want to keep this principle in mind as one of the building blocks of psychotherapy: how images are connected with emotions and how dangerous emotions can be without images. The first task of the therapist is to elicit images for strong emotions, even the emotion of depression. You can do this through dreams, storytelling, painting, and dance or body movement. I once did therapy with a troubled musician, sitting next to him on the piano, improvising bits of chords and melodies—musical images.

Jung's comment on images and emotions also suggests that it is not worthwhile to encourage emotional expression for its own sake. Just because a client cries does not mean that something substantial is happening. Or a wild scream of anger may release an emotion, but what good is that, except to be assured that an emotion is present? *Abreaction* has a place, but it is not the goal of therapy. When strong emotion comes along, you can look for the image in the emotion. If you have an image, the emotion will have meaning and you can deal with it.

The Therapist in the Jungle

Occasionally Jung used the word *contaminate* to describe being affected by powerful, raw material of the psyche. The raw stuff can be contagious, so that just being in the presence of it can affect your psyche. I remember one person I worked with years ago who was quite paranoid. I was a bit afraid of her. One night I dreamed that she came to my house with a weapon and threatened me. I took the dream to heart and did my best to protect myself from her paranoid thoughts. But she had contaminated me, to the point of appearing in my dreams.

A good therapist is not cocksure about dealing with the material of a disturbed psyche. She protects herself and is cautious around volatile material. A friend offering help would probably seek expert advice if he saw signs of psychosis. He, too, should respect the power of the psyche and its potential for overwhelming love and aggression. A disturbed psyche can lie concealed behind a soft and pleasant facade. So the rule is: always respect the power of the psyche for good and ill.

The drama of opposites enters here, too. The very person who shows you respect and admiration is the one who can reverse those feelings on a dime. This is a form of what Jung called "enantiodromia," opposites turning into each other. Seasoned therapists know that this drama of opposites can happen at any time, and still they might be shocked when it does occur. You get complacent with a client who seems so favorable and steady. The sudden shift into a very different demeanor can be difficult to deal with. So you have to be prepared, knowing from the beginning that any strong expression of friendly cooperation has its shadow, and part of therapy is to deal with shadow when it appears.

If the therapist cultivates a life of serenity and neutrality, she stands a chance against the wild beasts that are let loose in a psyche that has not yet found its fenced pasture. In medieval Europe stories were told of the unicorn, a beautiful animal that could cause widespread damage and yet was the very symbol of health. The image of the unicorn at its most useful showed him in a small pasture surrounded by a wooden fence. The psyche needs some containment, a fence or a vessel, to keep its wildness contained.

A therapist has the dangerous thought
That he does not want to get caught.
He has to think this thought
So he does not get caught.
Yet getting caught may be
his only chance
Of doing good.

Part 2

THE VESSEL

**The ego's pathology is inherently in sympathy
with the psyche's individuation.**

—*Patricia Berry (1982, p. 95)*

Therapeutic conversation is not ordinary talk. By selecting a good place, assuring confidentiality, and focusing on the psyche, you create a vessel, a closed, leakproof setting in which to engage in this special kind of reflection.

Chapter 7

BUILD THE VESSEL

The formality of therapy helps create what Jung called, using imagery from his long study of alchemy, the vessel. You need a tight vessel to hold the strong feelings that come up in the storytelling milieu of therapy. A coffee shop is friendly and warm, but not tight. Conversation there is usually rambling and without a definite purpose. There are many distractions, as well. A consulting room is formal and often effective at creating an airtight container for the expression of secrets and sensitive material.

In addition to the physical container, you need a vessel made up of attitudes, style of conversation, and agreements. You might assure your client or friend that whatever he says is confidential. You could show in a number of ways that you are trustworthy and can hold secrets. You can also not leave important items unsaid, like your assurances about confidentiality. But the main thing is to choose a place where you can talk privately.

In the practice of alchemy, the master uses variously shaped and sized vessels that hold the material to be treated and observed. The chemical reactions make colors and formations that, in the alchemist's eye, mirror the colorings and contours of human emotions and moods. Alchemy offers a system of metaphors for exploring human experience, and the vessel is essential. As many therapists do, I'm using it as a metaphor for how we provide a carefully formed container for therapeutic explorations.

Other considerations go into creating a good vessel for both formal and informal therapy. You have to be careful not to let anything you hear in private slip into other conversations. If you are not used to strict confidentiality, you may have to discuss it at some length with your client or friend so that you feel the burden sufficiently. The therapist has the task of keeping the vessel intact.

Confidentiality

Confidentiality, one of the essential means for making a good vessel, is less a technique than a strength in the therapist's character. Some people naturally keep secrets well, while others, though well-intentioned, tend to talk about private issues they have heard. Keeping a person's trust asks that you make a special effort and prepare yourself personally for keeping secrets.

If you have trouble keeping other people's activities and statements private, you might try developing your interior life more. Not speaking whatever comes to your mind is like closing a door gently to keep the noise out. If you're an extrovert, you don't have to become an introvert, but you can learn to appreciate the joys of privacy. The skill required is subtle, so you might start with your own material. See what it's like to be more private about yourself, and then apply that learning to another person's material.

You will be likely to break the vessel when your therapy conscience is too relaxed or not appreciated. You may not have learned forcefully enough the importance of confidentiality, or you may take it too lightly. Or you may worry about it so much that you can't make it an integral part of your identity as a therapist. You work too hard at it and so you have to be preoccupied with it instead of doing it naturally and gracefully.

The Room as a Vessel

One way I keep the vessel of therapy tight is to use my consulting room exclusively for formal conversations and writing. In my work there is not much difference between doing an hour of therapy and writing a book on the soul and spirit. When my clients enter our room, they know that it is a special place and that it is a therapy room even when therapy is not going on. The more you think through the choice of a special place, the better. You create a good vessel with imagination and intention.

Many professional therapists, I know, are conscious of how they decorate their consulting room: the colors, furniture, paintings and sculptures, and hangings. They may use a candle or incense to intensify the sacredness of the space. I have several special objects in my room that support therapy: a print of the Heart Sutra and of the Emerald Tablet (an ancient alchemical text), statues of St. Thomas More (my favorite saint) and Asklepios, the Greek god of healing. An old santo of the Virgin Mary, a photo of my grandparents and parents, a Native American ritual jade knife, images of the Buddha and Quan Yin, an obsidian stone, the collected writings of C. G. Jung and of James Hillman, sacred texts from around the world. I feel supported by all these presences that help me remember the sacredness of the work. They also go together to strengthen the vessel for therapy.

The Therapist's Persona

Other methods can help create the vessel. How you refer to yourself, how you dress, the way you talk about your practice or work, your language in general, your attitude and manner, your online presence, your correspondence style—all these create what today might be called a "brand" but also contribute to the nature and tightness of the vessel of your therapeutic work.

One thing I noticed about James Hillman was that he did not make a marked division between himself as therapist and himself as person. He did not hide his life or go to pains to maintain an aloof professional persona. If he was angry, he would let you know. If he was sad, he'd speak for it. So his vessel, though tight insofar as he treated therapy with utter seriousness, was not the same as his professionalism.

You knew that he was fully dedicated to the work, but he did not present it with any puffy formality. He cared about the soul, and in his presence you could sense his dedication.

Although my style is different from Hillman's, I have tried to avoid hiding behind a professional persona, too, while at the same time regarding the therapy process with seriousness and attention. These days I do most of the work online. I create the vessel by listening closely, keeping notes, cultivating a warm and genial atmosphere, and once in a while talking about myself. I don't want to be distant and hidden, but neither do I want to turn the therapy hour into a coffee chat. Because therapeutic conversations are so taut, so that every word has weight, the slightest deviation from form can create a leak in the vessel.

Maintaining the Vessel

In therapy I remember my tennis lessons. It does not do to just swing away at the ball. Of course, there has to be a degree of naturalness, but you also need considerable form. Bring that forehand back and away as the ball approaches. Swing with your body, not just your arm. So in therapy. Don't say whatever comes to your mind. Be aware of how your friend is feeling and what she needs from you. Think before you speak and watch your words. You need a combination of natural-ness and self-awareness, personal presence and professional technique.

In some ways therapy is an artificial conversation. I don't mean that in a negative way. I mean that you talk as though you were in a drama, where every word counts. You must understand that as therapist you have considerable power. The words you use are not the usual ones. They may be the same dictionary words, but in context they have an elevated standing. You must take care with them, because they can have more force than you intend and can either help or harm.

Once, in a conversation with a woman client, I wanted to be honest and let her know what I experienced in her presence. "You have strong opinions," I said. The next time we met she started crying immediately. "What's wrong?" I said innocently. "You said I have strong opinions. That's what my husband always said to me before we got divorced. I don't mean to be so strong. It's just who I am."

Obviously I was not aware of the meaning of my words when I used that phrase. I did not know they had a history, and such an emotional one. Now, there is no way to know in every case which words and phrases are loaded with meaning, but it would help to be cautious in your choice of words. The smallest judgment or criticism might be overwhelming to the person you're helping. Know, for instance, that even minimal expressions of love or disapproval can have an impact far out of proportion to your intention.

To put it more precisely, when you speak, often it is the archetypal figure speaking. Even when you are the informal therapist, a bigger figure uses your voice and you have added impact. The conversation may look quite ordinary, but once you frame it as helping, you're in the domain of therapy, informal of course. Most of the rules and observations about professional therapy apply, possibly with less force.

With Irvin Yalom's example in mind, I responded to

my client: "I did not realize that these words have so much meaning to you. Can we talk about them?" You can go on, of course, and discuss the offending phrase and explore the situations in which it was potent in the past. It's good material, but you have to be aware of how a person might be unsettled by a phrase from her past.

Words are never just terms from a dictionary. They are more like packaged time bombs ready to explode at the right moment. This power can be a positive resource or it can ruin everything. The main thing is to respect words and use them artfully. Understand that words don't always do what you want them to do. To an extent, they have a life of their own.

If you are careless with words and use powerful ones without thinking, you risk breaking part of whatever vessel you have been building. Words are like the two-by-fours or concrete blocks that form a wall and a structure. I am careful even with words of greeting and good-bye. You can ruin an hour of work by saying something like, "I hope we do better next time." That's a heavy judgment for a client or friend to carry for a week or so.

As a therapist you also have to watch what you say about yourself. If you say to a client when he's leaving, "I was not in good form today. I guess I'm tired," you're focusing on your own feelings of inadequacy and confusing your client. If you're worried about your performance, that is a good moment to be neutral by being silent. Deal with it later, preferably with a supervisor. A good therapist requires a skill that eludes many people: knowing when to hold your tongue. Doing so may help keep the vessel clean.

By the way, this means that the friend therapist should

understand that once you've agreed to lend a caring ear, you are in a new position. You are not just a friend now but a confidant. More than that, you are in a special trusted position that raises your status. Your words are now more potent than usual, so you have to use special care with them.

Remember your lessons from tennis or golf. You don't just swing your arms, and you don't just say whatever comes into your mind. Soul conversations are art forms requiring care and judgment. The therapy session begins with the first hello and does not end until your client or friend has gone. The time in between is, so to speak, in a glass container. Watch what you say.

Endings

Endings are particularly important—the end of a session or the end of a therapeutic relationship. The ending is like a potter putting the final strokes on a wet bowl. How you end can make all the difference.

My first rule of thumb is that therapy itself never ends. No closure. The client may find another therapist or another way to do therapy in the course of life. So I don't make a big deal of ending. I don't worry about closure. In fact, I'd rather end with au revoir than good-bye. Until the next time. I want to invite the client to keep thinking about doing therapy in some form. I have it in my mind and therefore in my words that therapy will definitely continue. I want to seed that idea at a time of ending: this is only a pause.

I assume that when a potter is finishing a job she does not

make a big deal of the ending. She's thinking of the next pot, and the next one won't be entirely new but for the most part a continuation of the work on the last one. Ending is to elide into the next project. It looks to the future. It's an amber light, not a red one.

Some long terms of therapy may ask for a little ceremony, but, still, I like to think of endings as musical cadences. A piece of music is full of many soft endings that are not final. Sometimes they are called "deceptive" cadences. You think it's over, but it's not. That's why some music ends with a bang, so you know it's really over.

Therapy is like that: you think it's over, but there is always the chance of another beginning. I like my therapy conclusions all to be cadences that clearly feel like endings and yet are not final. Let's be happy about life going on. Therapy is eternal and takes many forms. Remember the glass vessel, and be gentle with your good-byes.

The clear glass bottles
In an alchemist's laboratory
come in a set of many shapes and sizes,
A perfect metaphor for the kinds of
Receptivity
A therapist carries in his little black bag.

Chapter 8

LISTENING

In its earliest form, the word *listen* did not mean just hearing with your ears but more like "hearing" about someone. "Do you know who she is and what she has done?" In that sense a therapist or good friend listens to another to find out who she is, what is special about her. In this kind of listening you not only take in someone's words but also discover who they are.

Psychologists are trained to think in types and categories. Almost all have their own copy of the *Diagnostic and Statistical Manual of Mental Disorders*, in which various kinds of disturbances are listed, defined, and numbered. Most professional therapists can identify each of their clients with a specific number, and they can take classes, if they wish, in how to differentiate minutely one disorder, one number, from another.

When I am speaking therapeutically with someone, I am listening in a way that highlights hidden emotions and decodes language that says more than it is intended to say. I hear at several levels at once, and I pay more attention to undertones and overtones than to the direct message.

Reading James Hillman and classic Greek drama has trained me also to hear the voices of guiding spirits and gods and goddesses. In *The Iliad* and *The Odyssey* these spirits or *daimons* stand next to the heroes, advising them and leading them on in their destiny. I want to hear those voices, too, when I listen to a client narrate a life story or a recent troubling episode. I want to hear the voices of the inner critic and the influential parents, the voices of conscience and inspiration. I want to hear the mythic narrative that hums in the background of more immediate tales of woe.

When I was a music student in my earlier career, I took courses in ear training and orchestration, where I learned how to hear certain pitches and instruments and how to "hear" an orchestra by reading the score. I was shocked to discover that I was now hearing much more than I heard before the training. It was as if my ears had been washed clean and unplugged. Something similar happened as I became more skilled at therapeutic listening. Suddenly I heard more when I listened to a person talk, and that clarity in hearing became the foundation for becoming a good therapist.

Listening to Yourself

When I first began to practice therapy, I learned an odd lesson: not only did I have to learn how to listen to a client as an individual and at many levels, I also had to listen to myself. I had to listen to my overall story about being a therapist and to the patter going on in my head before and during a therapy session.

I could be talking to myself about how my day is going badly, how the financial side of my work is faltering, how many other things I have to do and maybe therapy is getting in the way. I may be discussing with myself how I feel about the client coming up next. These inner conversations could have an impact on how present I am to my client, and so it would be helpful to hear what I'm saying to myself.

In my thirties and forties especially I had a need to teach and counsel. I felt it was my talent and calling to be a teacher and a therapist, and I truly craved doing both. I felt a satisfying release and fulfillment whenever I had a chance to give a seminar or talk to a group or an individual about their life issues. It felt like a taut spring in me needed to be exercised and then relaxed, again and again.

Now I am older and feel different. I no longer have a need to teach and do therapy, although I still enjoy both and get a sensation of fulfillment when I do either one. Not needing these roles, I feel more free to engage other people and let them take what they can from me. I'm not as pushy as I used to be. Not as heroic and even as desperate. I feel energy for the work, but I also feel relaxed.

It helps then to listen to myself and find out where I am in my career. I know that I am no longer too eager, but I also know I still have a passion for the work. So I can go to meet my next client knowing that I will be present and still can listen intently. Having heard myself, I don't worry about being uninvolved, even though my passion is different in quality now, compared to my youth. Maybe this change is just part of aging, or maybe it is the result of experience. It helps to know myself before I start listening in a professional way.

I imagine these dynamics apply as well to friends and family members listening helpfully to each other. You may start with real enthusiasm for being available to someone you care for. But then, shortly into the conversation, you realize that it is not as easy as you expected. Soon you're out of your depth and you don't know where to go and what to do. You have to keep listening to yourself so that when the conversation is over you may be able to prepare better for next time. Do some reading or talk to a professional.

You also have to listen to yourself, both the professional and the amateur, to see if your subtle reactions are interfering with the dialogue. After all, you could define therapy as souls in dialogue. That means it is not just two conscious people talking. It is two people with complicated histories and highly tiered emotional backgrounds trying to be clear about matters that are essentially thick and cloudy. Your emotional memories might get triggered several times in the course of a single conversation. You know intuitively that you should not act on those triggers, or react. But it is not easy to keep your cool when one bullet of stimulus after another hits you where it hurts. As Jung said, clients seem to know intuitively how to get to their therapists and cause some damage. It takes a strong, aware person not to respond automatically and ineffectively.

You have to listen to yourself and once again remember your basic tennis lessons: Don't whack the ball. Pull your arm back just so and let your body bring full force into your swing. Don't whack your client or friend with your emotions. Listen to what is going on in you and use your basic skills and techniques in a conversation that is neither normal nor unconscious.

To be a good therapist you have to know yourself. Not perfectly and not self-consciously but deeply. I once had a therapist friend who was a carefree and wild spirit, at least on the surface. When he talked about his clients, I got the impression that he couldn't appreciate the more reserved and quiet ones. He told me how shocked he was at some of their inhibitions, and I thought to myself, *I couldn't be his client because I have those very inhibitions myself.* I wished my friend knew this about himself so he could be a more tolerant listener.

Everyone Has a Way of Speaking: A Rhetoric

Sometimes clients don't get into the formula for therapeutic talk that you prefer or consider appropriate. Several of my clients over the years have rambled on about events and observations with little obvious self-disclosure or attention to the inner life. Sometimes I have tried to steer the conversation toward a more analytical style, but to no effect. Gradually I learned to move with my clients in this regard and not expect them to conform to my idea of what is an appropriate therapeutic way of speaking.

When I get ruffled by the way a client is talking, I always remember a passage in López-Pedraza's book on Hermes. In *Hermes and His Children* (1977), he described a client who smokes a cigarette and rambles. Pedraza referred to this client's manner of talking as his rhetoric, his own way of using language. In the case he presented, he saw the god Priapus in play, a predominantly sexual god, odd, with no redeeming qualities, a freak and a scandal. Pedraza suggested that the therapist in this case be in touch with his own freakishness and then stay in tune with the patient's way of speaking, echoing it if possible. The idea is to enter into whatever complex has gotten hold of the patient through his style of language, his rhetoric.

My problem with clients talking endlessly about things that don't seem to matter is not Priapus but some other figure of banality, some god of everyday life. Some people prattle on. When they mention a name, they have to tell you all about that person, drifting further away from the original story. I don't try to pull a client away from this way of talking, because it is part of the myth, but I don't get caught up in it either. I don't veer off in my own preferred direction but rather stay observantly with the rambling and listen closely for any quiet indications of what the person is really trying to say. I have come to understand that rambling rhetoric is valid. It is the best way my client has to express her experiences.

Here and there I interject an insightful remark based on what I am hearing, which comes through like a peal of thunder. Occasionally a client, breathless from the meaningless narration, will say, "I wish you would say something enlightening." The client knows that he is rambling but can't help it, because his meandering manner of speaking is part of his symptom. He chides me for it, but that is just his way of voicing his impatience with himself. I'm careful not to get defensive and simply go on trying to hear a subtle message in the endless flow of words.

If you speak from your boredom, you are being too literal as a listener. A therapist never acts or speaks without art. You can never be completely natural, which is to say, unconscious. You are an artist of the psyche. You don't set the tone, you let your client do that, because in that tone may be a way deeper into the problem and therefore out of it.

You have to listen with your eyes as well as your ears. You notice gestures, postures, facial expressions, and body movements. There is never a moment in therapy when the situation is simple or one-dimensional. Many things are going on at once. You need all your senses at full power. Listening and watching go on seamlessly. You also have to be aware of your own multiple levels of involvement. Are some of your own memories being activated? Are your expectations getting in the way?

Often rambling and uninterrupted talk is obviously rooted in anxiety, and so it may help to do what you can to calm the person. I may invoke Carl Rogers, whose method can be magical in such moments. I sum up what I have heard and seen as accurately as I can. The person feels heard and witnessed, and she calms down. She may admit that she talks too much when she gets anxious, and that's a start toward a therapeutic conversation.

The Highs and Lows of Therapy

When I first considered becoming a therapist, I wondered if I was up to it. I had met several therapists who seemed to be fully in charge of life. They appeared confident, fearless, and all-knowing. I knew that I was insecure, entirely lacking in confidence, and shy. A turning point for me was a workshop I attended led by Piero Ferrucci and Laura Huxley. Laura was the wife of the author Aldous Huxley, and she was an accomplished violinist and a humanitarian who worked hard on behalf of children. She was a sensitive artist and I was a musician, and she saw right away that I did not fit in with the rough, overconfident therapists. Her simple recognition of who I was, her listening closely to what I had to say and what I could be, gave me the confidence to become a therapist in my own right.

Later, of course, I saw through the bravado of the hero therapists and recognized their hidden self-doubt. They no longer stood in my way. I never lost all my deep-seated insecurities, but I managed to find a life of self-confidence and leadership anyway. I have empathy for those who are called to be therapists even when they feel they are in serious need of therapy themselves.

Today I often run into people who are the opposite of the wild cowboys that bothered me. These people are clearly troubled, insecure, and mousey. I ask them what they do, and, somewhat surprisingly, they tell me they are therapists. I don't know what to think. One thought, not at all charitable, is that these are the people who really need therapy and deal with that need by becoming therapists. It's a switch that I can understand. Maybe I had some of that in me early on, as well. I understand and treat them as colleagues and assume that they will also arrive at a place of confidence and strength.

Wherever you are on this spectrum, you can listen with

empathy to someone unburdening himself and offer modeling and leadership. You don't have to be perfect, but you need some confidence and at least the illusion of personal strength. Although you are in touch with your frailties, you have to listen as someone in a better place. Your friend does not want to hear about your problems or past failures. She needs the image of you as strong and in charge, not confused and suffering. This useful subtle deception could be Hermes, a little duplicity for the sake of the therapy. You may not be feeling all together and strong, but you may find these qualities in yourself for your client.

There is an honest paradox here: you can be strong only if you are in touch with your weakness, and sometimes you can be honest about your state of mind by showing the complexity of your emotions. The cowboy therapists were strong on the surface but were out of touch with their weakness. You can show your weakness without sacrificing your strength. A measure of self-doubt keeps your strong position honest.

The Imperfect Patient

Sometimes I listen with a degree of paranoia or suspicion. Is the client purposely leaving out important details? Has she asked for my help but then decided not to give me any reliable information? Is she being seductive? If she is, should I listen for further meaning in the seduction? Should I call her on it, ignore it, discuss it, or try to understand it at a deep level?

You can be paranoid and trusting at the same time, if you

allow yourself some distance from the thoughts and feelings coming up in you. You remember that you're not an ordinary person in this relationship. You are the therapist or a friend in a good position to help. It won't hurt the relationship to wonder about her sincerity or honesty. As a therapist, you can expect a client to be dishonest. That's material. It's part of the complex you're helping with. If your client is perfect, what is there to talk about?

Therapy does not require full honesty. It would be better to hear the story with all its protective shields and misdirections than a tale cleaned up for therapeutic use. As a therapist you cannot be naïve. You have to expect shadow, expect to be manipulated. It's all right. This is a basic human effort to risk telling a story by getting to the real facts slowly, one at a time. You can't do it perfectly or purely. Only a moralistic therapist would expect unalloyed truth. A soulful therapist does not ask for purity but only a valiant effort to be present.

I wish, I wish I could be right.
I wish I could do everything well.
I wish I could listen perfectly.
But my wishes brown and curl
Like leaves at the end of summer,
Like clouds appearing at the end of a clear day.

Chapter 9

GETTING STUCK

Years ago a client came to me and sat down and did not say a word. I greeted her and suggested she tell me her story, but she sat still and quiet. From the very beginning of the therapy we were in limbo. Sometimes the therapy gets to a place where no progress occurs and it seems there is no point in continuing. You may take this feeling as a sign to stop, or you could also see it as an essential part of the process.

Often in the course of therapy a client will say, "I feel that we aren't getting anywhere. I feel frozen. This isn't working." The therapist may be alarmed. He is not doing his job. What's wrong? Has he lost his skill? Is it his fault that nothing seems to "work"? In rare cases, maybe that is exactly what is happening. But more often it's simply the dynamic of the therapeutic flow, which includes moments of empty waiting.

Naturally, the same thing can happen when a friend is counseling another. The lay therapist is not trained to deal with such an unexpected development and may be tempted to give up. But even in informal helping conversations, the helper might have patience and the strength to continue. Getting stuck or feeling like giving up is common even in deep conversations where the people are really committed to the process.

Just Waiting

Waiting is a skill in therapy that you don't find explored much in training programs, when you do nothing and feel all right doing it. Personally, I feel comfortable waiting, maybe because I've long been devoted to the work of Samuel Beckett, author of *Waiting for Godot*. Beckett raised waiting to the status of an archetype. Many people wonder who Godot is. To me the matter is simple: Godot is whoever and whatever we are waiting for when we wait.

Beckett's play is about waiting as such. It is an activity that has little of the hero in it and much of the antihero and therefore is close to soul. Imagine an action hero in a modern movie saying to his nemesis: "I'm going to wait you out." How would the film proceed? Who would want to watch ninety minutes of waiting?

In therapy the problem may be that you think mechanically about an issue involving the soul. You think of yourself as a machine that can break down and needs to be fixed. If you had to wait a week to get your car fixed, you might feel frustrated. *What's taking so long?* But the psyche is not a machine. Running into problems is its modus operandi. Everyone has emotional issues at least sometime in their lives, most of us every day. If you take the mechanical approach to your soul, you may wait anxiously for things to return to normal. But what if, in the big picture, there is no normal? Then there is nothing to wait for.

Another way of having nothing to wait for is always to be waiting. Waiting is, as Beckett saw with unusual insight, archetypal. Human beings know the feeling of waiting, even if they don't know what they're waiting for. It would help a therapist to sort this matter out, because feeling stuck and not getting anywhere is common in therapy and can discourage both patient and therapist.

Again Beckett is right on with his insight. When you understand that waiting is the human condition, then there is nothing to be done. In my work I have used this four-word mantra as a guideline—Nothing to be done. And yet we can work at issues in such a way that we aren't hell-bent on getting somewhere. We can relax in the timeless environment of the psyche. Again, the *Tao Te Ching* is a good guide here: "The wise person does nothing and teaches wordless lessons. The ten thousand things come and go without his doing." I can be actively involved in the therapy without the intention of accomplishing anything and even believing that nothing is getting done.

No Need for Change

In therapy, you may reach a point where you realize that what you thought to be a time-bound life problem is something deeply lodged in the person's soul. This may be the reason why you feel stuck. There is no real future if what you thought you could change now appears to be your essence. It won't go away. You are tossed off the linear conveyor belt of time. Suddenly you may realize that there is "nothing to be done because I am both okay and not okay the way I am." Essentially I am not going to change.

Maybe your client does not need to change as much as you think. Or maybe it would be better not to think of therapy as having to do with change. You are distilling the essences, making an essential oil out of a multitude of experiences and influences. Therapy, as Jung thought, is a kind of alchemy. The primary job of the alchemist was to wait and watch, to concoct a potion and not to solve a problem.

If alchemy has a goal, it is the *lapis philosophorum*, the stone of the philosophers. Not an actual stone, but a hard, firm, lasting quality of character. (*Lapis* is Latin for "stone.") But why a stone? All that work on one's past and confused emotions and busted relationships ending up as a stone? Why that metaphor? Maybe because we're after something natural, long-lasting, tough, resilient, and weighty. Furthermore, to all appearances a stone does not move, and if and when it goes through change, no one perceives the movement. I've come to think that that's what people are like: when they do go through changes, often you can't see them. They're stones.

You could define the hero as that figure in us who feels driven, at all costs, to do something. The Taoist sage is quite different. He is the therapist who accomplishes much by doing nothing. That means not acting with heroic intention and expectation. Therapy may "only" bring you to a new vision of yourself and your situation. You are not going to change, but you can still do something, or not do something. If you have recently seen more clearly who you are, maybe now you can be that person—a matter of being, not doing.

Discovering Your Essence

Therapy may move you away from the wish to change, even if change was your aim in going into therapy. Your purpose becomes more subtle. You may realize that your problem, the very core of your neurotic ways, stood in the way of your essence because you could not see how to translate it into life. You may have undervalued it and misconstrued it. It may have had shadow in it that you did not know how to reconcile.

I once sat with a woman who was eager to change because she did not like the person she was. "I haven't done anything with my life," she said. "I want to accomplish something before I die." So should I help her run through the possibilities of what she could do to satisfy her longing? Should we get engaged in a practical strategy of change? I did not think so. It seemed clear to me that it was her demand on herself that was her real problem. She could not let her deeper self show through because she had a fixed image of what a successful person looked like. I felt we had to be less active, not more active, and let her soul be revealed. You can't work hard at becoming somebody if you aren't somebody to begin with.

The discovery of your essence, or at least a sidelong glance at it, can be felt as stuckness. You can't move on because you can't see a goal or even a direction. You keep trying one explanation for your life after another. Each may sound convincing, but they fail to take you anywhere. You're still in the same place, and it does not feel like progress. Then you may get an insight: Maybe progress is not the way to go. Maybe you have to stop for once and simply be who you are. Maybe even your past, with all its mistakes and embarrassments was essentially you and acceptable. It could be no other way.

The path out of being stuck is to remain stuck. Not getting anywhere allows you to feel what the experience of yourself is like. I have been talking about essence, and yet Aristotle would say that your essence is your soul. So let's rewrite what we have been thinking through. We get stuck in order to feel the soul's presence rather than the flow of life. In the realm of the soul you don't change but perhaps orient yourself differently. You don't flow, because your essence is the still point in your existence. The feeling of being stuck is a sensation appropriate to the soul. Marsilio Ficino (1975) said, "The soul is partly in time and partly in eternity." The part that is in eternity requires a meditative pause, a point of view apart from the flow of time, and maybe even the annoying sensation of being stuck.

Getting stuck could be a symptomatic form of attaining nirvana. Samsara is the flow, nirvana the pause. If we follow our rule that a symptom points to what is needed and should be preserved so that we know what we need and have access to it through the symptom, then getting stuck points to a far deeper and positive way to not make progress. Nirvana.

I have been reflecting on this paradox for years: You know you are not the person you'd like to be now. You're chronically angry, you get jealous, and you can't get your work life on track. You need to change. And yet the deepest and most reliable sources, like the Taoists, say you don't need to change.

Could it be that you are fine being the person you are, but you have rough elements, what Jung referred to as *nigredo* material, that are raw and need to flower? If you try to change, these raw materials may not come to fruition. Then you will only have more of the *massa confusa*, not a good situation. So don't change. Sit there, reflect, read poetry, and let your soul emerge. Soul emergence is the biggest secret of them all.

I can imagine two followers of Zen or Taoism in therapy: "We aren't getting anywhere." "Good. Finally."

One way not to get into the state of nirvana is to become absorbed in the culture. The cycle of births and deaths that describes *samsara*, what nirvana saves you from, is the meaningless, thoughtless, standard life: unconscious consumption of material things, assumption of thoughtless values, diminished appreciation of intelligence and wisdom, the pursuit of mere entertainment instead of pleasure, disregard of meaning and purpose, the avoidance of fate and community. Nirvana is withdrawal from this mindless and immature escape from honest living.

Of course we get stuck, because we need to pause and be free of the urge to do. We're stuck in therapy because we need a radical overhaul. Habits and assumptions run deep, and we are not liberated from them without a midpoint of loss. We need to let go of the old ways before we can take on a new viewpoint. A familiar Zen story tells of the teacher filling the student's cup with an overflowing amount of tea, a lesson about having some emptiness, some space for developments, some stuckness in our feverish activity.

Both therapist and client may have a samsara mind-set in their otherwise good work. They're busy trying to do something and to arrive at a goal. If they are not making progress toward that goal, they feel stuck. The problem is not so mysterious. The problem is the goal and the busy attempt to arrive at it. A flower does not need a goal. It just blossoms.

So in therapy you allow the feeling of not getting anywhere to hover and do its job. Don't fight it or make it better. Don't think that you know how long it has to linger. Let it work on both of you, client and therapist, until it finally fades from lack of interest. If you stop asking why you feel stuck, the feeling might go away. You discover that you have been asking the wrong questions.

If you go with this symptom of being stuck, you will stop trying to get somewhere and pause in your feverish hyperactivity. You will finally exit the hero myth that is so unconsciously embedded in modern life. You will learn how to be and not just do. At that point therapy can begin, so in a sense your conversations lead to the point of stuckness. It is their goal.

Medusa and the Horse

Patricia Berry, the brilliant Jungian and archetypal analyst, has written about Medusa as an image of being stuck. The gorgon turns a person to stone. She became pregnant by the water and horse god Poseidon, so that when the hero

Perseus killed her with his sword, out came the horse-child Pegasus, whose hoof dug into the earth and made a spring, Hippocrene (horse-spring), from which come inspiration and creative ideas. If you drink from this spring, you will be blessed by the Muses.

Berry sees the birth of Pegasus as a gift of the gorgon's curse of stuckness. This myth would have us consider that within our immobility is a pregnancy and possibility for unusual creativity, a close connection to the Muses and to the deep, earthy kind of inspiration, the kind that bubbles up from the depths and offers certainty and confidence. And so waiting may be a gestating, carrying to term that asks for near impossible patience.

A story is told of Beckett sitting in a theater watching one of his own plays. A companion said, "There is some hope." "Oh no," said Beckett. "No hope at all." There can't be any hope, because it would destroy the purity of the waiting and the absoluteness of being stuck. You can't cheat by believing in an end to the waiting.

Being stuck in the context of therapy can take many forms: "I'm not getting anywhere. I'm wasting my money. I need a better therapist." A good therapist recognizes the genre of this bit of theater. Being stuck. She also knows, now more than ever, that patience is in order. A horse of creative power is getting close, waiting to be revealed. There are no guarantees, and you can't outwit the pattern by clinging to hope and expectation. You have to know about Pegasus without demanding that he appear. His birth is a gift of the gods and especially the petrifying goddess who has snakes for hair, the goddess who makes time stand still.

Being hopelessly stuck and having profound creativity burst onto the scene are two necessities. They go together. You can't rationalize their processes and explain how they work. You just trust that stuckness is allied to new life. In the myth, Pegasus, the artistic horse, springs out of the head of Medusa, the petrifying monster. Out of your snakelike despair can arise a powerful, animal-based creativity.

All this work and I'm getting nowhere.

But nowhere is a cool place.

Nothing going on here,

But lots of life.

Could I have been looking for nowhere

All this time

And waiting for nothing?

Chapter 10

THE MIST OF CHILDHOOD

Stories from childhood are usually more potent and useful than other stories you tell. You see patterns there that still operate in you as an adult, and you get the feeling that through these stories you touch the very roots of your being. They are odd because they seem to be about the past and yet give you a good picture of who you are now.

Sometimes, when people tell stories about their childhood, they quickly get to blaming their parents for their problems. Most of us take these stories literally and think that our parents and certain key experiences in childhood are the *cause* of adult problems. But both Hillman and Jung warned against taking childhood too literally. About the child archetype Jung (1968) said: "The child motif represents not only something that existed in the distant past but also something that exists now; that is to say, it is not just a vestige but a system functioning in the present whose purpose is to compensate or correct, in a meaningful manner, the inevitable one-sidedness and extravagances of the conscious mind" (p. 162). This is a key idea: "memories" from childhood are not vestiges from the actual past but images coloring the present. They are not history but filters for seeing certain aspects of what is going on now.

Let me use myself as an example. When I was a child I was a quiet kid who did not talk much and was not loud. Sometimes now when I remember back to that silence and my current problem expressing myself in certain situations, I explain that my mother frequently told me to be quiet. Her word for a badly behaved child was *bold*, and I was not supposed to be bold. It is a convincing explanation.

But as an adult I enjoy being quiet and I love solitude. I don't think that comes from my mother wanting me to be quiet. By nature I seem to have a contemplative character. It's basically a positive quality, and it certainly thrived when I lived in a monastery, a life that I loved and look back on fondly. So maybe the story about my mother is inaccurate, taking my childhood experience literally and blaming a parent. It might be better to understand that from the beginning I have been a quiet person, and although I can easily connect my solitude as an adult with my childhood, the one may not be the cause of the other. Being quiet as a child tells me who I am rather than what happened.

As a therapist I'm careful, then, when a client talks about his parents or childhood, not to hear it as it is told, as a literal story about what happened and how those early events are responsible for who the adult is today. I have copied the sentence from Jung that I quoted previously and reread it now and then. I want to remember that the child and childhood are filters, translucent images for looking at present situations.

Certain archetypal or mythic images are more easily transparent for us. We can imagine the hero, the magician, the warrior, and the huntress, say, as images and not as historical figures. You may sense immediately, for example, that Joan of Arc represents young female courage and leadership. We are more interested in that image than in how her actions had an impact on history, one that continues to this day. But an image of our own childhood—in stories we tell, in old photographs or in therapy discussions—seems so factual and real that we find it more difficult to see it as an image. We take it literally and see childhood as the cause of current turmoil. We focus on history rather than archetype.

Recounting our childhood certainly says something about our background, experience, and character, but raising the image of the child also introduces feelings and fantasies about new life, new beginnings, and new being. The child appears, say in dreams, to announce a new development that may challenge, as Jung said, the status quo. The child is a living image, in and of the present, not only a historical fact. I emphasize the imaginal child because ordinarily we assume that talk about childhood is personal history.

Therefore, when a child appears in a client's dream, I may look to see if some new development is making an appearance in the dreamer's life. I might ask, "Does this beginning make you feel like a child? Do you feel inept, raw, or clumsy? Or creative, hopeful, and excited? Can you sense that special sensation that a new phase of life is under way?"

I have heard many dreams of older people that take them back to school and adolescence, the older child. In actual life they may be starting a new job or making a big turn in life.

They may need new skills and information. So the dream puts them in school once again. It is as though they were in elementary school or college, depending on the nature of the current new development.

At times like these adults may feel like a child or young person again and relive the sense of feeling inexperienced and uninformed. The spirit of the child is visiting. It may arrive many times during a person's life, because it is not limited by time. The child is always with us, at times more pressing than others.

James Hillman (1975a), who also wrote extensively about childhood, said: "We cannot know what children are until we have understood more of the working of the fantasy child, the archetypal child in the subjective psyche" (p. 10). Stories about childhood told in therapy are the soul speaking through the image of childhood. Because imagination is always at work, there is no way to know childhood except through current thoughts about childhood.

In general, Hillman defined memory as a form of imagination. As you remember what life was like as a child, you are reimagining your past life and returning to a child's way of seeing the world. The child is always present but comes to the surface at the appropriate times.

Fictions from Childhood

The stories we tell today about our childhood may feel like precise history—the facts clear, the emotions remembered well, responsibilities given to the right people. And yet there are many signs that, to put it in Hillman's strong language, our stories are also part fiction. Tell those stories in a gathering of family members, and you will hear corrections and variations. Hear yourself tell a story from childhood more than once, and you may catch yourself telling a different version of the tale. Those variations express your current reality, maybe the way you think today.

You tell many different stories, based on the same facts. There is the story a person has told for years and has given life its meaning. The therapist may want to guide his client to a new story about the same events, one less damning perhaps or not full of blame. There are other variations, but these two may cause a struggle in therapy. The client is attached to his story because it is familiar and keeps things calm, while the therapist believes that the story he can imagine is healthier. No one is right, but the counterpoint, or clash, can be liberating.

I remember one person who blamed her father for the misery of her life. She was firm in that narrative and did not want it to change one bit. After hearing her story many times, I felt a little compassion for her father. At least, I could understand from his background how he might have been a bad parent. I had the idea that if she could find some opening to her father, just a sliver of understanding, she might be released from the hatred that made her a bitter person. For a while we had competing narratives.

In the end, with this client I felt that, although she did not come over to my version of events, the conversation loosened up the rigid story she had been telling all her life. Our therapy took the form of the alchemical *solutio*, the breaking up of a tightly wrapped image of a life into its parts. Getting cracks in her story was a partial solution, at least, of her problem. She felt the *solutio* as a solution, a resolution of her issues. She knew she had more work to do, but she ended the therapy at that point feeling transformed and able to approach her life with less bitterness.

This, by the way, is an example of an ending that is strong but not final. I felt somewhat incomplete and would have liked the therapy to have continued, but I understood that after intense work to reach that point, the woman wanted to live for a while without facing new narratives for her experience. She now had a revised version of her childhood that felt liberating to her. Still, she and I both knew that future revision would help even more. Naturally, I trusted and respected her decision, and it would please me, for what that is worth, if one day she called and said she would like to go back to therapy. I suspect that she will find another therapist and pass the baton. That would also feel good to me.

Therapy as Literary Art

A passage from the poet Wallace Stevens (1989) has guided me for many years in my understanding of both religion and depth psychology: "The final belief is to believe in a fiction, which you know to be a fiction, there being nothing else. The exquisite truth is to know that it is a fiction and that you believe in it willingly" (p. 189). These words are not as radical as they may sound at first. You just have to accept that everything we say is colored by the limits of our understanding, our emotional biases, and our hopes and wishes. Imagination shapes everything we say and think. Whenever we tell the stories of our lives, we are all novelists.

In his book *Healing Fiction*, Hillman (1983) went further. He said that therapy offers the opportunity to opt into a better fiction, tell a more advanced story about your life. You may especially include less blame and less slighting of important figures. You may appreciate the complexity of the novel better than before. You may tell your story with more imagination and insight and less raw emotion. Your complexes may play a softer role, and you may be more forgiving of yourself and others (p. 26).

This is a key for therapists and for friends guiding friends: Try to get to a more sophisticated story about your client's or friend's life. Aim for less obvious blame and for more compassion toward parents and other major figures. Learn that life is always more complicated and subtle than you have usually imagined it. Revise your stories, make them more mature and precise, and clear them of strong childish emotions.

The Child of the Soul

The child of the soul is quite different from the child of memory. The historical facts are not as relevant, for one thing. This child is eternal, *puer aeternus*, as monks chant at Christmas, a festival honoring the birth of this soul child. Jung said that the child of the psyche announces new beginnings. At those moments when your life is taking a fresh turn and something new is starting up, you may dream of a baby. This is not a child of time but a set of qualities best imaged through your experience of a child. This archetypal child drifts into awareness, an expression of the freshness of your experience.

Young married couples often behave as children, filled with the spirit of new beginning. They may reveal the degree of joy, hope, and playfulness they feel as they look out on a new phase of life for each of them and for their marriage. The day you start a new job a similar child spirit may arise in you. It may not last as long as you thought it would, but just being there offers an impetus to life and the bounce you need to be optimistic. These are gifts of the child of the soul, which plays an important function in the dynamics of an ordinary life.

But Hillman, ever the spokesperson for shadow, reminded us of another side of the child we might overlook. The child can be colicky, needy, dependent, capable of hair-raising tantrums, whiny, and dirty. These qualities also come with the soul's child. You may not be able to have one without the other—the creative spirit and the whiny complainer. People who smilingly speak of their "inner child" often overlook the child who throws tantrums.

So let's not confuse the important archetypal child, the herald of new life, with the sentimental idea of an "inner child" that is adorable. New beginnings, imagined through the image of a child, can be difficult. There may be fears and tantrums and the feeling that you can't walk or talk like an adult. Both sides of this child experience have value, and usually you can't have one without the other.

The Adult-Child Split

When we find ourselves in a childlike episode, no matter how old we are, we may run into an obstacle, a harsh adult voice from within or without. A corresponding adult figure may show up to keep the child spirit in bounds or to criticize and punish. Archetypal images often come in twos. Part of a complete therapy would include coming to terms with this child spirit and taming the adult negativity about it. The free child elicits a constraining adult, a conflict you may feel internally or in relationships. The child plays freely and the adult lays down the law.

If you have surrendered to the culture's demand to grow up and behave like an adult, you may have a negative reaction to your own child spirit when it appears. You are expected to grow up, not to act like a child. Or, as often happens, the child spirit erupts in you and you hear the voice of a parent telling you to act like an adult. Most of us have been taught to tame that child and finally snuff it out.

A person in therapy feels strongly about something that is said and cries. Then she apologizes for crying. It could be the child coming to life in the weeping. The woman thinks, *I should not cry. I'm an adult. I should face these things stoically.* The frail child has appeared, and with it the negative adult.

At a moment like this, one therapeutic response is to silence the punishing authoritarian and be kinder to the archetypal child. That kindness might carry over to the child of personal history. We talk about blaming ourselves for various things, but to be more precise, often we are chiding the child of the soul. Adults are often impatient with children being children, but they also find it difficult to be around the archetypal child, the child of the soul that appears in them and others.

Consider giving the child more room in your life, allowing yourself to be more dependent and ill-behaved as a price for spontaneity and creativity. You can also help your serious adult become friends with the playful child by actually playing more games and being physically carefree in adult situations. In a split like this, the two sides can each give something to the other. You could more often be playfully serious and seriously playful. Or you could work hard for a few hours and then play with abandon. There are many ways to keep child and adult on good terms with each other.

A therapist or soul friend has to be careful not to fall into the role of punishing adult in response to a client's child spirit. That is to say, the adult-child split archetype may be apportioned between therapist and client. The client brings forth the child spirit in some way, and the therapist gets caught in a countertransference by which he either plays with the child or corrects it. It is better to keep the pair intact and in a good relationship. No splitting. But as usual it is the therapist's job to notice the splitting and to do something about it.

Fully Adult and Still the Child

I remember some of the private times when I got to know Hillman better. Once, we were at a play and his mother sat next to me, telling me some stories about "Jimmy's" early years. James was on the other side of me, wincing. I was quite pleased, hearing about the childhood of someone who did not believe in it. As happens to us all at times, his mother did not let him hide his child and maintain his extreme adult persona.

Another time, we sat wearing our swim trunks in the indoor spa and hot tub at his house in Connecticut. He complained of the breasts he was growing in his old age. I wondered about this further extension of his person, now into the weakness of the androgyne, as Hillman's friend López-Pedraza described it. James was a bit embarrassed about who he was becoming, but I felt it was the appropriate softening of a personality, a further identification with the mother.

A few years later, I sat next to him for a long while as he lay in a hospital bed that had been placed in that same spa room, morphine dripping into his body to control the pain from his untreatable cancer. On both occasions I was moved to hear him speak with candor, confessing his love of life. I also noticed, as I spent a few hours at his bedside, how several people came to say their last good-byes, each of them telling him that they loved him, this man who was a terror to many, who spoke his mind, and who wrote with great passion for the ideas that stormed into his imagination. These were his children, I felt, coming to the mother and father in James, a touching completion of deeply felt relationships. I felt that James dealt with these "children" with kindness and understanding.

Hillman taught me that you can be incisive in your analysis of culture and people's lives, point out the shadow when they would prefer to take a sentimental, shadow-free approach, and goad them to grow up and be strong. At the same time you can enjoy simple optimism and love everyday things, like baseball. You can be very adult and very childlike, not seeking a balance but enjoying the extremes without splitting them.

Hillman wanted people to live their lives boldly and not hide behind their neurotic parents. He was interested in the archetypal father and mother, both of whom he wrote about. He wanted to see through the actual parents to the deeper family myth playing out, because he felt there was freedom and individuality in finally reconciling with the Great Mother and the Great Father.

Leaving Childhood, but Not Leaving It Behind

Jung said that one of the chief tasks of therapy is to help a person leave childhood and become an adult, to be part of the world instead of being stuck in the dynamics of the personal family. Yet, he said, we need to keep our roots in the family so we don't lose touch with our instinctive feelings. We have to break with childhood and yet remain there, too.

We are always shifting from one avatar of the archetypal parent to another: from teacher to spouse to the boss on the job to the minister or priest to the president of any organization that supports you. At any one time I feel that I have twenty-five mothers and fathers spread around in my world. You can release yourself from bad memories of childhood, enough to move on to archetypal parenting.

You keep moving toward adult independence and yet you become more involved in the archetypal family.

You can spend years scanning the world for appropriate and effective "mothers" and "fathers." You have to be both connected to your family for a foundation and discovering new kinds of parents and siblings in the big world. It is not a bad thing to keep finding parents everywhere. You need them. They are a gift. Yet they may come with complications every bit as knotty as those of your actual parents. Clearly, this is a complicated process and one of the most important in your soul care. A good therapist has to sort out for himself the tight connections between the actual and the archetypal parents before guiding someone along its twisted and rocky path of being an eternal child.

The therapist has to spot the moment when the client or friend begins thinking of him, the therapist, as a parent. It is not always determined by gender. Men make good mothers, and women can father effectively. This is not a bad thing, but it does bring with it specific problems. You have to be especially careful not to identify with the parent and let your patient slip into childhood. Let him or her be an adult and parent you for a change. You can be a child in your therapist's role and let your client be both mother and father to you.

Jung warned against transferring the child-parent feeling to a government or to the culture. You might act out the child in relation to a manager or politician. You would have given away too much. Instead he recommended the "kingdom within," a reference to the gospel teaching as a way of life, where the father is in heaven, while the son is on earth. Read the Gospel of John closely and psychologically, and you will notice that the father's celestial realm, though involved in this one, is never confused with worldly life. We should never confuse the real-life parent with the archetypal one.

If you are a parent temporarily relating therapeutically to your child, helping her sort out her emotions, you have to take special care to separate your childhood from hers and your mythic child from hers, as well. You can allow your child to live her own life and have her own experiences. This can be a rule in your philosophy of parenthood, and if you don't have such a philosophy, it's time to start making one.

Jung (1966) wrote, "A person's philosophy of life guides the therapist and shapes the spirit of his therapy. . . . It may and very likely will be shattered time after time on colliding with the truth of the patient, but it rises again, rejuvenated by the experience" (p. 79).

When you're talking to a child, you are an adult. There is a natural distance between you. Remember that speaking to children is an art and should not ever be a spontaneous, unconscious act. If you forget they are children, you will likely treat them from your unconsciousness. Listen to an adult trying to correct a misbehaving child. What is that tone? It is not normal or human. It is a complex rooted in the split archetype of parent and child. When you are with children, you may have to make a conscious decision not to speak from a parent complex. Otherwise, the connection will not be clear or real; your voice will serve the parental complex that has you in its grip.

You, the therapist, may be the first real parent your client has ever had. Or you might be the best avatar of the parent archetype. Your client, like everyone else, needs a multitude of parents in the course of a life. You would be doing your job well if you could be the channel for the archetypal parent and make that gift to your client. You would be a special, translucent parent who represents and ushers in the Great Father or Mother.

Children have much to unlearn
As they grow up and enter
The adult world.
Education is forgetting
Until they mature
And begin remembering
Once again
Where they came from.

Part 3

SOUL STUFF

Do you know love-nights?
Do petal-cups of soft words
drift in your blood?
Are there not places
on your lovely body
that remember
as if they were eyes?

—*Rainer Maria Rilke, translated by Thomas Moore*

Work with the psyche is not the same as managing life or solving problems. It goes deep and looks for underlying narratives and themes. Dreams help reveal those themes that are currently in play, but you can also spot them in stories from daily life.

Chapter 11

DREAM WORK

It's a mysterious thing, yet nothing could be more ordinary: We go to bed at night, fall into a state we call sleep, and then visit lands of nearly pure fantasy. We revisit people from the past, those who have gone before us, and people we never knew. We do things that contradict the laws of nature, like flying in the air by flapping our arms. We have nightmares that make the heart pound with fear. Then we wake up, saying we "had" a dream, when actually we were in a dream.

In dreams I am a participant. I sense a continuity between the person I am in life and the dream-ego, the "I" experiencing the dream. Yet the dream-ego may be quite different in other respects from who I am in waking life. I meet a friend there, too, who in most respects is the same person I know in life, yet he may do something entirely unlike him. He feels like the person I know, but he is clearly someone else. He lives in the realm of dream.

Scientists say we don't dream the whole night long, but

nevertheless we spend a third of our lives asleep and a portion of that in dreamland. During the day we are also in a kind of dreamscape. With just a little attention, we can perceive a deeper story being lived out beneath the facts of daily life. I meet a man who reminds me a little of an uncle. Suddenly my relation to him is more dreamlike than factual. My family myth comes to life, and with this man I am in an old dream.

We are a rare society that does not take dreams seriously. Many intelligent people in the past have used dreams to help them find their way. Patricia Cox Miller (1994) wrote that close to two thousand years ago dreams "functioned to bring submerged thoughts and fears to conscious awareness and provoked the dreamer to new forms of interaction with the world." They "were barometers of inner dispositions and as roadmaps for negotiating the intersection of personal conscience and public action" (p. 252). The fascination with dreams that many people have today is no doubt a reaction to the failure of society to take them seriously. We are now hungry to reconnect with this deep country of the psyche that promises to resolve many of our problems.

For centuries brilliant writers have explored theories about dreaming and methods for dealing with them. People have used dreams for divination and have understood them as visitations by angels and other spirits, hints about the future, and patterns from the dreamer's psychological life. Freud published his *The Interpretation of Dreams* in 1900 to mark the beginning of a new century and a new era, when the deep, dark realm of the unconscious would be explored with new dedication. In the very first sentence he (1965) wrote:

" . . . every dream reveals itself as a psychical structure which has a meaning and which can be inserted at an assignable point in the mental activities of waking life" (p. 35). Notice: every dream is meaningful and relates to waking life.

For many years I have focused my therapeutic work on the dreams of my clients. I don't have many theories or methods, though I have been strongly affected by Hillman's (1979) book *The Dream and the Underworld*, in which he recommended that we enter deeply into a dream and be affected by it, rather than translate the dream into the terms and concepts of waking life. We should not interpret dreams but rather be interpreted by them, he said.

I don't want to interpret a dream so exhaustively that it is explained and done with. The dream should always remain a challenge with its impenetrable images. At the same time, within that scope, I use everything in my power to help uncover some meaning: mythology, literature, psychology, etymology, my client's associations, my own associations, and encyclopedias of knowledge. I think we can throw everything at a dream, as long as we don't kill it with conclusive interpretations.

Just recently I had a brief dream that felt meaningful to me. My twenty-six-year-old daughter, who is a creative musician, had layers of gauze about two inches square on her forehead, and blood was seeping through. Her mother would take one piece of gauze after the other away, and the blood again gushed out. At first I wrote that she had a cut on her head, but the dream did not show that. All I know is that blood seeped through the gauze. It's important to be as precise as possible in recounting the dream.

I thought about the dream first as having to do with my daughter. She has a strong maternal instinct that encourages her to take care of people, sometimes at her own expense. I thought the dream might show how blood, possibly an image for heart and caring, pours out of her in the area of her mind and imagination. There is a way in which the mind can bleed. But she can't take care of herself enough to stop it (mothering of herself is not effective). There is something wrong with the blood because there is medical gauze over it.

To focus in on the dream, it would help to have a few dreams from around the same time period. Dreams often arrive in batches, relating most of the time in theme and imagery and sometimes in meaning. Jung (1966) wrote: "I attach little importance to the interpretation of single dreams. . . . Later dreams correct the mistakes we have made in handling those that went before" (p. 150).

In my dream of my daughter, I could imagine the entire drama taking place within my own psyche. Jung might have said that it is my anima, my daughter anima, that is bleeding profusely. I, too, have a tendency to bleed my emotions and especially to think therapeutically, in a caring way. I've never forgotten a professor of mine saying once, "Tom, your trouble is that you are pastoral in your approach to life. You don't have enough distance from events and people." That blood pouring out of my daughter's head could be the pastoral Thomas Moore, the one whose thinking is perhaps colored too much by his exaggerated compassion. For myself, I like to be therapeutic at all times, even in my writing. My head bleeds for my readers.

Often a dream will contain two or three different scenes

yet seem to be a single dream. It could be that the various scenes make the same point in different imagery and maybe with different emphases. In the first part of a dream a woman encounters an attractive man she'd like to get to know. In the second part she is taking care of a baby in a park she loves. Both dream elements may point to new life for the dreamer: one, a new wonderful figure coming up in her life, and two, the baby as a sign of new life.

Professional therapists of all stripes could study dreams and bring them into their practice. You don't have to be an expert. Just don't be overly certain about your reading of it. Think of your role as adding some reflections but not offering a final interpretation. Soon you will discover that dreams can give you more insight into a person than the stories they tell.

These days I often work a dream with a group of people. I set an example by not reaching quickly for an interpretation but rather offer reflections on various images. The group follows me and carefully gives their responses. We talk this way for half an hour and then gently leave off. We have come a good distance into the dream but we have not "nailed" it.

A therapist might also pay attention to his or her dream life, because those dreams could help maintain an awareness of issues in play beneath of the surface of the work. The dreams might offer hints of how the therapist is interfering with the therapy and directions to go in the work. One great advantage is that dreams are current. They give you a view of things as they are now, not in the abstract.

If I were to take the bleeding, bandaged head as a sign about my current work as a therapist, I might consider that there is too much blood coming out of my head, my thoughts and purposes. Maybe it needs some drying up, a little less compassion and more insight.

Let me offer just a few guidelines.

Guidelines for Dream Work

Notice where and when the dream takes place. Sometimes it is a clearly marked period in the dreamer's life and sometimes it seems outside of time and place. Always think metaphorically, not just literally. If the dream is at a school, consider that the dream may be reflecting a learning situation. The dreamer may be in "school" learning about a new area of life.

Notice over time certain themes that keep coming up in dreams. For several years I had dreams of commercial airliners trying to take off from crowded city streets. I did not have "room" to "take off." With dreams you can put quotation marks around many words, pointing to the metaphors. Once my writing "took off," I stopped having dreams of airplanes. Now, looking back on those dreams, I feel that to get my ideas and work "off the ground" I need more space for myself, less crowding of cultural ideas and the things I had learned from others. You can probably tell from the style of this book that I could still benefit from reflection on that dream and write more from my own ideas and experience than from the crowded space of others.

Many modern people have trouble with dreams because they don't usually think metaphorically. If they were to look at more paintings or read more poetry they would be used to thinking at multiple levels that are accessible only through metaphor. If you have a habit of noticing metaphors, you can get a great deal from dreams without resorting to many techniques and theories.

When I first talk with people about dreams, I often hear from them various ways they'd like to get a handle on a dream, so they can use it and dispel its mystery. "What about lucid dreams?" someone will always say. "Or anima and shadow in dreams?" "What does a snake mean in dreams?" "Are dream figures all parts of myself?"

These are all good questions, but notice how they all want to limit a dream instead of remaining in the presence of a dream's mystery. It is more effective in the long run to practice Keats's negative capability and tolerate a dream's resistance to interpretation. Stay in the mystery of it as long as you can, even as you try to make some sense of it.

One of the main skills you need when you work with a dream is patience. I need a full hour with a dream. If, fifteen minutes in, I still have no idea what the dream is about, I just wait. Over time, with probing and open-minded conversation that is not hell-bent on a final interpretation, the dream almost always reveals itself. Most of the time you will finish the hour with a good, confident sense of what the dream might be saying about your client.

Dreams reveal more than a person's life stories do. They often act like x-rays, showing what is beneath the surface and invisible to the naked eye. Yes, they typically speak in obscure metaphors, but once you peek behind the images you feel as if your eyes have been opened. You see what both you and your client have not been able to perceive with all your mental efforts.

You begin to trust the dream. Often my most intelligent and experienced clients, many of them therapists themselves, leave a session saying, "I had no idea there was so much waiting for me in that dream. I just did not see it." Sometimes it takes an eye that is not clouded by hope and fear to behold the message from the night drama. Many people say that it's easier to find meaning in someone else's dream than in your own. Could it be that dream work is one of those human activities that we have to do with another person?

In my workshops I usually spend an hour each morning discussing a dream or two that someone in the group had the night before. I have come to trust groups and appreciate what they can offer a dreamer. I find that I can add some technical insights to the dream, but members of the group each have responses that are unique and valuable. I manage the discussion lightly so there is no analyzing of the dreamer. I keep the focus on the dream images and point out when the response is too symbolic and explanatory. I ask for reflections, not interpretations. The conversation is not headed for a conclusion but always hovers over the dream.

Whether individually or in a group the essential thing is to stop using your hyperactive intelligence to pin the dream down. You have to be receptive, wait for the dream to show you its meaning, put some reins on that demanding intellectual ego of yours. Be more relaxed. Let the dream give you thoughts. Don't force it into the open. It's a special skill to allow thoughts to arise into awareness instead of forcing them through mental exertion.

As I mentioned at the beginning, I have often thought that if I could create my own graduate department of psychotherapy, I'd have mythology, art history, world religions, poetry, and depth psychology on the curriculum. You have to study and prepare yourself to deal with images, including dream images. You need an ear for narrative, lyric, tragedy, and absurdity to catch the drift of night dreams. If you come to the practice so prepared, you might notice in dreams the deep dramas being enacted beneath the surface of an ordinary life. You appreciate theatrical, mythic, and poetic images that move from dream into life.

How Not to Interpret Dreams

Most of the instructions for dream work are too heroic. They are determined to blast the dream open and reveal its secrets in plain language. It might be better to approach a dream the way you might walk into an ancient temple—with reverence and an appreciation for mystery. Rather than explain the dream, you might instead bow down and allow the great mystery to be uttered in a sacred tongue, a language that you will devote yourself to and appreciate.

One word associated with dreams from ancient times and still used by some today is *incubation*. This word, of course, is used for birds sitting patiently on their eggs, waiting for them to hatch. What a perfect image for dealing with dreams. Sit with them patiently and keep them warm until they are ready to open up and reveal what they are all about.

Some suggest "dreaming the dream onward," remaining

in the realm of the dream as you gradually enter waking life. Draw, paint, or make poetry of your dream. One of my clients always gives a dramatic title to a dream, a way of bringing strong imagination to his encounter with the dream. Or you can remain in a half-dream state when you talk about the dream, instead of aiming directly for clear explanations and applications.

Without any interpretation a dream can be beneficial. It can deepen your point of view and teach you how to see metaphor everywhere, which is like perceiving the dream nature of everyday life. It can help you appreciate the nonego elements in your sense of self and understand that you are a community of persons living in many different time periods at once. It can make you a poet to your life, reading everyday events as you would a dream. It helps you understand that you exist on many levels, some of them mysterious and unfathomable.

Let the dream interpret you. Let it affect the way you think and express yourself. Let it give you a glimpse of its mysteries. Let it give you the language to use and the meaning to cherish. Let the dream teach you to be dreamier, more reflective, and in some ways less active. Become a priest of the dreamworld, not its conqueror. Allow the dream to make you less forceful and analytical, more poetic and imaginative. The ultimate goal in dream work may not be interpretation at all but in the invitation to live more fully in the realm of dream.

Jung once remarked that your dream work is not finished until you notice what it is asking of you. He used a stronger phrase: an ethical demand. After I had my dream of my daughter's bleeding head, I thought about her current life. She is embarking on the demanding career of a touring musician and music producer. I see her studying hard, taking difficult courses, and working long hours. I put that image into my reflections on the dream and have changed my style of doing therapy a little. I am being more analytical and more challenging than usual. I'm getting blood from the head and not just from the heart. I also have to be careful not to let my passion be too contained in my head. The dream seems to show that something is wrong with blood oozing from my bandaged head. With a dream, you are rarely certain about the final interpretation. You accept all the various ways of understanding it and allow a response to emerge.

I walk through the caves of dream
And phantasms whirl around me
memories fall like rain
And I see myself as in a mirror darkly.

Chapter 12

COMPLEXES

If you have ever been in the presence of someone who is better read, traveled, or skilled than you, then you probably know what it's like to have an inferiority complex settle on you and cause you considerable discomfort. The complex takes over and makes you feel and do things that just are not you. You may start blabbering, making excuses for why you are not more traveled. I do it all the time. You may feel possessed. You can't get rid of the feeling no matter what you do.

Jung placed complexes at the heart of his psychology, describing a complex as a "splintered psyche" or as a fragment of the psyche, highly emotional and—the key quality—autonomous. A complex acts like a person inside you who can take possession of you and make you feel things you wish you did not feel. It can also give you a good picture of what is going on deep in the psyche. This is an important clue for therapy. Complexes are not things to get rid of directly. They are a doorway to the entire psyche, and so therapy pays close attention to them and respects them.

Of course, people want to be free of their complexes, but the route to freedom goes through the complex rather than against it or around it. You feel your inferiority, let it be, and ask yourself if this complex tells you what you need. Do you need some humbling? Would you be better off if that inferiority complex gave you a more accurate picture of your abilities and talents? You may believe that entering into the complex will sink you into low self-esteem, but it is more likely that it will give you a more realistic view of yourself.

Complex and Archetype

Hillman described the complex as held within the shell of a deeper archetypal pattern. That means that your feeling of inferiority, say, is shaped at one level by your experiences and personality, but beneath the personal lies a basic human sense of being less than perfect. The archetypal level brings even deeper emotion and more penetrating meaning with it.

You may have noticed that many people are susceptible to feeling bad about themselves for not having an ability that someone else has. To do therapy deeply enough, you have to touch upon the archetypal. You can have compassion for your client, knowing that it's a very human thing to feel inferior. It is not his fault, because it's not personal. Blame keeps everything at a superficial level.

In the sixteenth century the theologian and humanist Erasmus wrote his famous book *In Praise of Folly*, showing the many ways it is useful to be foolish or even just to feel foolish. For one thing, he said, it brings you down to the level of the rest of humanity, in case you are feeling too good about yourself. This inspired book spells out the archetype of the fool and is an example of taking what could be anyone's complex and revealing its paradoxical value. Erasmus was doing what I am suggesting: finding significant lessons in a symptom.

Sometimes complexes come through, as Jung said, as a voice inside you, or a presence that may feel overwhelming. You may feel like a different person, or possessed. After doing something embarrassing you may say, "That just was not me," or, "It was not like me to do that." To "get caught" in a complex is to be at the mercy of its emotion and compulsive energy. You can do nothing to keep it at bay.

Another example is jealousy, a basic human experience, but you may be particularly devastated by it because you don't want to be seen as a jealous person. You may wish it away, but you have to learn some key secrets about relationship before it will retreat. A good therapist respects the power of this complex, knowing its archetypal strength, and yet also knows that it can be dealt with effectively over time. It can fade away as a bothersome complex as it gradually morphs into a basic truth of relationships.

A life lesson first appears as a symptom—you feel inferior. Eventually you realize that it is all right not to be perfect or to know everything. But this deep awareness may arrive only after several experiences of the symptom, feeling inferior. Getting free from a complex can take years, and so the therapist has to be patient and help her client be patient. You may not notice when you have learned the lesson deeply, and when you're not looking, the symptom fades away.

Don't Defeat the Symptom

As always, the purpose is not to defeat the complex but to slowly transform it into a valuable quality. In the case of jealousy, the good part might be effective dependency that does not hurt you. But it could take a long time to transform raw jealousy into gracious vulnerability. And the complex may never go away completely but rather remain as a source of further deepening.

A young man recently told me about his helping complex. He lives in San Francisco and walks the streets almost every day. If he has money in his pocket, he can't help giving it all away to people on the street begging. Sometimes, to avoid the problem, he does not bring money with him.

The man has a helping complex that arrives when he encounters someone in need. He can't not help, even though he's giving away money he needs. This complex is especially difficult because his action looks like a good deed. As is always the case, a therapist has to be careful not to get caught in the apparent virtuousness of the behavior. Is it not always good to give money to the poor?

What should his therapist do? Don't tell the man he has to take care of himself and ignore people who want money from him. Trying to will the complex away only makes matters worse. Suppressing the complex often looks benign, but it's really a heroic attack on this fragment of psyche. Anyway, plain willpower is no match for it. A complex may have roots that dig deep into the psyche. You can't just extract it. Instead, you could see this "problem" as an opportunity for this man's life to expand.

You might ask him to tell you in detail what happens when he feels compelled to give away his money. Just to describe the problem in general terms is not enough. You need a narrative, images, details. When you hear the full story, you may notice certain subthemes worth pointing out and discussing. The clue to a complex may be something small and easily overlooked. That's why you have to be sharp and catch tiny clues hidden to an ordinary eye.

Suppose you were to ask this man what happens when a street person approaches him. He says, "I feel like I'm privileged and don't deserve to have money in my pocket." You ask where that idea came from. "From the nuns at school. They taught me that it's good to be poor and bad to have money." You say, "But you don't have much money." "It makes no difference. Compared to the man on the street, I'm wealthy."

So here we have material for conversation, and the therapist can take this material deeper by deftly steering the discussion. For one thing, childhood is in play. He mentioned the nuns at school. And we just discussed the child archetype in some depth. Maybe this man has to develop a more adult attitude toward money and replace his childhood story with a more mature one. Religion also plays a role with its moral demands. They can last a lifetime. He may also need some spiritual maturing, an assessment of values he picked up from nuns when he was a child. This could be a project in itself.

So we have rich material for opening up this person's

money complex and his need to help. There is no single-statement solution, but the narratives that could emerge, added to a dream or two, should be enough to make progress with the symptom. A complex does not puff up and blow away, it unravels, showing what is inside it and giving you material to work with.

Where Do Complexes Come From?

In the example of runaway generosity, the symptom is connected to religion or spirituality, which often exhort people to be generous to a fault. Remembering our discussion about countertransference, you, the therapist, might pay attention to your own attitude toward this symptom. You may be thinking, *I have the same problem.* Or, *I have no difficulty ignoring street people. How could he be like that?* Either attitude is probably your own unconscious response to your friend's issue, your own complex related to money and giving. In that case, we have dueling complexes, and that can be an added problem.

However, Jung points out that if a therapist can't deal with his own complex, he won't be effective with someone else's. So another interesting response would be to focus on your own issues about giving money away. Given that money almost always has a complex connected to it, you could focus some attention on your own issues. That would bring you closer to your client's problem in a way you can understand and maneuver. Of course, you have to be careful not to confuse your own touchy matters with your client's, but that is something you always have to do.

You could also ask for a recent dream, which might give you a hint as to the roots of your friend's complex. In dreams these hints may not be obviously related to the issue. Let's say the man dreams that a child asks him for a cookie, and he says, "No, sugar is not good for you." In a topsy-turvy way this dream may be a commentary on the man's problem with beggars. The dream suggests that the man may not be as generous as he thinks.

Remember that a complex tells us what the soul needs and points to a solution. This "generosity" complex could point to this person's potential to be more generous. The automatic response to the complex is to correct it—help the man stop giving away his money. A more subtle and wiser approach is to wonder how he might be more giving, in a way that does not hurt him. The complex hints that he's not really being generous on the street. He's acting compulsively, against his will. He could face this unconscious lack of generosity and consider ways to give to others willingly and sincerely. He could "reach out" more to people in need.

As a complex ripens into a psychological strength, the language about it may change. In serious jealousy, for instance, first you are afraid you'll lose someone you love. It's probably not just the person you worry about but the whole experience of intimacy. You feel as though your very existence hangs on the relationship, and the jealousy shows that your very foundations are threatened. It is not just about relationship but also about feeling alive and having a source of meaning. That is one reason why it makes you feel so desperate and shaky.

When the jealousy finally leaves or diminishes, in its place will be not something new exactly but a ripened version of the jealousy. You will have learned that you can be vulnerable and trusting without threat to your existence. Jealousy transforms into mature and comfortable vulnerability. None of us can ensure that someone we love will always stay with us. Jealousy and secure love are opposites, one transforming into the other. You may learn that you can't expect any one person to save you from your basic aloneness in life. Your complex may bring you eventually to a less neurotic way of relating.

As a complex it is jealousy; as a resolution it is the capacity to be vulnerable and allow the other the freedom to choose you. Jealousy is a powerfully destabilizing condition, but it is an opportunity for becoming more mature about love.

A Complex Can Be Beneficial

As I already mentioned, a complex can be contagious. A client tells you about her jealous feelings, and you are reminded of your own tendency to be jealous. Memories and old emotions may surface in you. This is a form of countertransference but with a slight twist. You identify with your client and have to face your own difficult emotions. Obviously this is material for your own therapy or supervision.

The practice of therapists to discuss their cases with a psychological supervisor is a brilliant idea. If only people in other fields had such an opportunity—police officers, business leaders, politicians, doctors. It is an example of one of the basic rules of life: we need each other. Often we need another person because we can't do a certain task by ourselves. This is certainly true of noticing where and when our complexes appear and interfere with our work.

The main problem with a complex is that it is cut off from other elements in the psyche that would restrain it and modify it. As Jung said, it's like a splintered self using your body and your life to get what it wants. In this separated state, the complex amasses such power that you may not be able to control it. You have to recognize it for what it is and bring it down to size. But it does not work to try to get rid of it. You have to make indirect moves that allow it to transform and ripen.

A complex can sometimes serve you. Jung (1966) wrote, "A complex does not in itself signify neurosis, for complexes are the normal foci (locations) of psychic happenings, and the fact that they are painful is no proof of pathological disturbance. Suffering is not an illness; it is the normal counterpole to happiness. A complex becomes pathological only when we think we have not got it" (pp. 78–79).

On a number of occasions I have asked a group of nurses how many of them had a mother complex. The majority said yes. They had converted their mothering complex into a profession of care. Even so, of course, their complex may get away from them at times, and some may still have a problem with being too maternal. But the rule holds: your complex can serve you if you can find the right outlet. You can also tone it down that way, making it less autonomous. You can't make this conversion perfectly, but the task is not to wipe out a complex. You can render it more human and able to fit into the whole of your life.

Jung described a complex as a split-off part of the psyche and then went on to suggest integrating it. I hear people talking about integrating a complex as if it's a job for a Saturday afternoon. It sounds easy. But Jung consistently presented it as a highly emotional, complicated procedure. He said that whereas formerly you found the complex out in the world, once you integrate it you may have to deal with it in yourself. Our client may stop giving money away too freely and then feel that he has to help everyone in need. He may become a therapist and have an overwhelming need to help his clients. You can alter a complex without fulfilling its core, and then you are still at its mercy.

The complex is so deep and serious that you have to devote yourself to its transformation. I often hear from my clients that they are surprised how deep the therapy goes and how fundamentally they have to reorient their lives. Of course, no one changes essentially or entirely, but a complex may be so intrinsically rooted that only a significant change will affect it. From a certain point of view, therapy is a religious practice because it touches on the essence of who you are. You don't just adjust your emotions, you do what you can to affect your very being.

I can imagine our client, who cannot help but give his money away, in the end discovering that he has a calling to serve humanity, and his complex may lead to a remarkable way of life, giving generously to the world—his small complex realized in a big way. Sometimes a complex that shows itself as a personality problem is resolved into a spiritual dedication much greater in scope. The solution is the enlargement and perfecting of a small personal issue into a serious contribution to society.

Sometimes a complex,
A soul person,
Will stand next to you
Like another you
Who is quite other.
Or sit inside you
Quite loud and demanding
Needing a home.

Chapter 13

HOW INVOLVED SHOULD YOU BE?

In 1935 Jung gave a series of lectures in London at the Tavistock Clinic. The audience consisted of medical people, psychiatrists, and artists. The Irish writer Samuel Beckett came with the noted psychoanalyst W. R. Bion, who was his analyst at the time. Jung gave five lectures, and in the last he talked about countertransference in strong terms. Here is what he (1976) said about patients: "They always find out this vulnerable spot in the analyst, and he can be sure that, whenever something gets into him, it will be exactly in that place where he is without defense. That is the place where he is unconscious himself and where he is apt to make exactly the same projections as the patient. Then the condition of participation happens, or, more strictly speaking, a condition of personal contamination through mutual unconsciousness" (p. 141).

This was obviously spoken by a seasoned analyst with perhaps a trace of bitterness. From what Jung had to say about transference you get the impression that he struggled with it many times, and we know that his professional life and his personal life often got tangled. He frequently used the word *participation* to mean a loss of awareness and necessary distance and a sinking into a blind passion, whether love or hate, usually love. In transference you are a participant in a melodrama, and you don't know what it's about exactly or how to get out of it.

So, yes, therapists have to be cautious about getting caught in the complexes of their clients. One complex I often see in daily life is the overwhelming need to be a mother or parent. Recently I almost cut my finger while chopping vegetables. Two people nearby couldn't stop asking me if I was all right and offered all sorts of remedies. I *almost* cut my finger, and the complexes rushed out. Others present apparently did not have this complex and went about their business.

It would be tempting for many people to feel a similar need to help when a friend appears worried and distressed. You may need to help more than your friend needs help. You can step in, but know your complexes. Understand that you may have a tendency to overdo the caring attitude. That does not mean you shouldn't help, but only that you have to be cautious with your complex.

Every moment we live with and through our complexes, certain powerful needs and longings that are more like inner persons than mere feelings. You can't be without them, and they allow you to live a productive and dedicated life. But they easily get out of hand and out of your agency. The emotions of a complex are your own reactions to events to the tenth power. You are no longer directing them and allowing them to be an integral part of who you are. A complex can become a devilish Mr. Hyde to your sweet Dr. Jekyll.

Fear of Involvement

This is one side of the issue, the danger of getting caught in a complex, which I have dealt with in some detail in the discussion about transference. The other side is fear of involvement. In therapy circles there is a corresponding and equally disruptive anxiety about being close to your client or friend. The theory seems to go: if I keep a distance from my client, I won't have an inappropriate relationship and I will be able to say what needs to be said without fear of offending.

But there is a well-known dynamic at work here that puts this approach into question. If you actively avoid having any intimacy with your client, you may well push that energy down into your unconscious and force it to erupt as a big problem. It's possible that the rules given to therapists to avoid contact actually increase the possibility of extra-strong attraction and troublesome behavior. Those who want to maintain the chastity of therapy might promote conscious closeness and in that more direct way avoid the erotic problems that sometimes emerge. When they make eros a crime, they are probably making it more appealing, as well.

On reflection, I think what has helped me are two basic attitudes toward the work. First, I love the soul of the person I'm working with. Even if they are very different from me or if I don't like them or disapprove of their behavior, I still love their souls. Usually I don't need or want a personal relationship. Second, I always try to normalize the context of therapy. I don't make the situation precious or surrounded by heavy rules or self-consciously separate from ordinary life. I try to be just who I am. I'm open to friendships with the people who come to me. That is just being human. And I think these two attitudes, love of soul and normalcy, have helped me more than anything to keep a proper boundary.

Now, having laid down two principles, let me add a third suggestion, related to the first. I am in love with soul work. It is my passion and consumes almost all my waking thoughts. I am a full-time soul worker, and that dedication blurs any other attractions, especially those that might have a negative impact on the work. This focus, I believe, keeps me away from any personalizing that would only get in the way.

Therapy involves intimate conversations, which could lead to problematic intimacy. It's easy to confuse therapy love for personal love. I think of therapy love as agape, the kind of love Jesus and the Buddha taught, a high evaluation of the other person as a human being and a heartfelt connection.

I'm not saying that eros has no place in therapy. Attraction can give the therapeutic activity drive and tenacity. But if it spills over into sexual expression, the free and uncluttered vessel can be broken, or at least cracked. I don't want to be a moralist about this issue. As I said before, I'm sure there are conditions in which sexual expression could be compatible with therapy. But that would be rare. I suggest getting deep pleasure from close work with another person's soul.

Aphrodite as the Goddess of Therapy

Once again let me evoke Aphrodite, the Greek goddess of sexuality, sensuality, the beauty of nature, and especially the sea, gardens, and coupling. The spirit this mythological goddess embodies is fully present today in all these areas. You can certainly sense the special atmosphere when you step into a lush summer garden or find yourself in the presence of an extremely attractive person. That atmosphere, experienced both inner and outer, is what the Greeks tried to capture in their stories, rituals, and images of Aphrodite, and we can still feel her presence, even if typically we don't use her name or engage in her formal rituals.

One of the great problems of our time is neglect of this particular goddess. Interestingly, the Greeks often warned that if you neglect any deity, but especially this one, she will seek her revenge and set things right. The way Aphrodite responds to neglect is to cause intense and often problematic desire for love and romance.

We neglect the demands of the Aphroditic passions and therefore suffer her revenge, in the form of extreme preoccupation with sex and a compulsive interest in pornography and extramarital love. We fear her and can't fit her into our usual ways of thinking about life, and then suffer her revenge. We also witness our difficulty honoring her in a cultural loss of grace and beauty. This is true of the institution of psychotherapy, as well. We surround therapists with demands for sexual purity, whereas we could instead do everything possible to make the profession exquisitely caring and those in it beautiful people of grace and loving-kindness.

Aphrodite might be the spirit that moves us to be more involved with our clients, instead of maintaining a protective distance. Going forward toward a more positive connection with them we may fend off sexual confusion and uncertainty about the nature of the relationship. Allowing Aphrodite a place in therapy might help define therapeutic love, which is its own kind of closeness. It does not tend toward sexual expression but, just the opposite, does not want any obstacle to the therapeutic work. It so appreciates the person open to doing the work, and the soul work itself, that personal indulgence in eros is not so tempting.

Close and Distant

The therapeutic relationship, formal or informal, has two important dimensions. One is a willingness to be close to another person as she explores some challenging, perhaps painful emotions and entanglements. Even if you are paid for your service, it is an act of generosity. The main instrument of your work is your own self. By establishing and deepening a relationship, taking some responsibility for what goes on, you are offering the person the chance to move further into life and, you hope, ease the pain. You work by being connected to that person, showing her what Carl Rogers called unconditional positive regard.

The other dimension is a certain distance that allows you to reflect on the stories your client tells. He is too close to events to see clearly what is going on or may not understand well how life works. Therapy involves education as well as emotional clarification. It's difficult to deal with a challenging human situation if you don't really know, at a meaningful level, what is going on. A therapist usually has a more sophisticated and more objective point of view.

Both closeness and distance are important, and it may be better to find ways to do both rather than to find a middle way between the two. Generally, I don't favor the idea of balance. Life is rarely balanced, and then only intellectually. I prefer to think of a therapist as sometimes being both intensely engaged and sometimes, maybe most of the time, standing back far enough to see what is happening. In the best of circumstances, you can do both at once.

I often find myself expressing my empathy, how I appreciate the pain and confusion, and in the same breath I try to clarify matters. Emotionally I am the same way: deeply engaged and standing back. Overall, I want to be part of this person's life, someone she can call on at odd times for support, and also the therapist who is not suffering the problem and may have something to offer from a distance.

The Therapeutic Angel

I go back to the notion that the real therapist is the Therapeutic Angel, the archetypal therapist, whom I conjure up through my education, experience, and studied way of conducting a therapeutic session. To be the magus who brings the archetypal therapist into the consulting room, I need some distance from the person in my care. If I am too involved, I can't put on my ritual robes, to speak metaphorically, and invite the

Therapist in. The personalistic atmosphere of a too-close relationship does not make room for this angel.

Outside this intense ritual place of therapy, I go on with my life, finding as much joy and meaning as I can, knowing that my independence and personal happiness make me a better therapist. But in my own time I may think about a client now and then and even jot down a few notes or write a brief email. I keep somewhat soft boundaries between my life and my work. Once in a while a situation calls for hard borders and I try to maintain those with love.

I'm careful to distinguish a therapeutic friendship from personal friendship. I may feel a real friendship with a client, but usually that does not become a personal friendship outside the therapeutic vessel. On occasions a personal friend will ask for a therapeutic conversation, and I do it, finding simple ways to maintain borders. Sometimes a client will become a friend. That is often the case, and there, too, we keep the two forms of friendship separate. I like walking into the therapy room with a friend, who then gently but clearly morphs into a client. The setting and timing of therapy helps maintain the distance between the two relationships.

As a therapist you are both shaman and neighbor and can comfortably play the two roles at once. It may take a little imagination, but that's what your education and training are for. You don't want to be sexually or romantically involved with a client, but you do want to be therapeutically involved.

If you're devoted to the soul and to your job as a caretaker of soul, you should not be tempted to stray from that role. It takes all of you to do that job, and you won't want anything to interfere with it. When I was a monk, I lived a life of celibacy, and I have always believed that such a life was possible for me, even in my early twenties, because of the intensity of the community life I experienced daily. It's similar in therapy. The deep and intimate joy of soul work does not leave room for any personal sexual or romantic needs. The work of intense care for souls keeps my heart busy and full.

Don't worry about being close to another person
But know your need and craving
So it does not distort being close
Into possessing and binding
Or letting loose your emotions
That have been in bondage
Because you haven't known how
To be close to another person.

Part 4

THERAPY IN THE WORLD

As the hearth fire of Vesta, which is of wood, require careful tending and do not have anything spectacular about them—just a warm glow; small community activities and projects, generated by the people by themselves; heterogeneous lifestyles, comfortable in conversation with each other; street cafes, places where people can sit—legitimately lazy—be on view and watch the world go by . . . rites of utmost importance, entrusted to the Vestal Virgins.

—*Robert Sardello (1982, p. 104)*

Therapy can happen in everyday situations that don't look like therapy: education, parenting, and simply being friends. At work and in business dealings, people often console and encourage each other. The soul is to be found in the thick of life, and where soul is so is psychotherapy.

Chapter 14

CARING FOR THE
WORLD'S SOUL

You can't stay with the neurotic culture, buy into it fully, and at the same time live a soulful life. You can't find happiness when the things around you are unhappy and you can't expect emotional problems to resolve if your soul is sick, and the world's soul, too. If you are a therapist, you can't see the planet suffering from pollution and do nothing.

My point is that we can all find ways to be the world's therapist. My wife is an artist reaching out to the whole world, conscious of the beauty in cultural diversity. My daughter sings in a visionary way with the conscious intention of helping young people avoid the usual addictions. My stepson practices architecture in a way that will help communities thrive. My father was a plumber who taught his students how to set up elegant pipe systems, skillfully welded, to keep water flowing in buildings and homes. He also taught them values of character and responsibility so they could do their job well. These are just a few of my family members, and each one is or was a therapist to the world. Imagine how many people out there are doing informal therapy.

People make jokes about bartenders and hairdressers listening to their woes, but this is truly a form of therapy, if quite informal and far outside a professional format. Once you get this idea of informal therapy in the world, it's difficult to imagine a job that does not have some therapeutic potential. Therefore, I don't merely advocate therapy for the world but also therapy in the world.

Objects Are Subjects

I was born in Detroit, Michigan, a city that, when I was growing up especially, was known as "Motor City," a hub for automobile manufacturing. I have always had an interest in cars, but today I'm interested in the cars that appear in dreams. The fact that cars frequently appear in dreams shows that they have a connection with the soul. In a dream the car may suggest being taken somewhere, if you are not in the driver's seat, or being in control, if you are. There are other possibilities, like associating a certain year and model of car with a period in your life. When people talk about cars, that's how they sometimes think. A person might say, "Oh, yes. That was the year I was driving an old VW Bug. It was not a good year."

In a certain way, a car has a soul. You know this from

the affection people have for certain automobiles. Care of the automobile's soul might lead to a more humane way of buying and selling them, making them in a way that truly harmonizes them with other important social values like environmental concerns and making them financially accessible to more people. Making them beautiful, ornate, and pleasurable might also lure some soul into them. More power is probably not a way toward the soul of the automobile, but it may account for its spiritedness. I look forward to the day when a major automobile company hires a psychotherapist sensitive to the world soul to assist in the design of cars.

The soul may benefit from a design that echoes the natural world, is rich in detail, and is colorful. Notice how computers, so focused on information and intellect, tend to be hard-cornered, smooth, and colorless. I have suggested that we restore a nineteenth-century sensibility and put bird feet on their bases or paint them with forest scenes. At my desk I use a richly detailed William Morris mouse pad to help keep nature and soul tied to my computer. I can appreciate a modern sleekness and coloring in style, but I'd like to see a return to the Morris and Edward Burne-Jones sensitivity to the beauty of everyday things. Morris, who was certainly a therapist for the world, wrote: "Have nothing in your house that you do not know to be useful, or believe to be beautiful." Edward Burne-Jones was even more romantic: "I mean by a picture a beautiful, romantic dream of something that never was, never will be—in a light better than any light that ever shone—in a land no one can define, or remember, only desire . . ."

Therapeutic Design

We are in psyche; psyche is not in us. The way we order and shape our world profoundly affects how our soul is either fed or starved in daily life. When we put a richly detailed and beautifully designed mouse pad on our desk, we are inviting soul into daily living. It is a small act, an apparently physical one of little importance. In our house, when we want to wrap a gift, we don't go to the store. We use a sheet of soft Japanese paper with calligraphy on it that my wife has been practicing on. Suddenly the gift seems beyond price. If we do many such acts on behalf of nature-inspired beauty, we are tapping into the soul of things.

Making a soulful world is also a therapeutic act. We are caring for the world in a way that increases its beauty and depth, gives it personality, removes the shallow and hard objectivity that is so characteristic of our times, and restores a relationship of appreciation and intimacy with the things that are not so much our possessions as our friends. Designers and architects have a special opportunity to restore soul to a world very much in need of it. I look forward to a major shift in taste, away from hard-edged glass and steel to soft, detailed, organic, and extravagant design.

I made the point earlier that friendship can be the principle or basis on which we relate generally to people, even in brief and commercial encounters. The same could be said of things. We could stay close to them emotionally and keep the ideal of friendship alive. When we treat things badly, we are setting ourselves up for a loss of soul, with all its attendant symptoms and problems. It may sound strange to say it, but when we are feeling depressed or anxious, it could be that objects in our environment are suffering, and we are feeling their distress. We could correct that important relationship through what may seem to be an odd kind of therapy, caring for things and befriending them.

Early in my career I was sometimes linked with the popular homemaking guru Martha Stewart. The references then were often derogatory, and I can just hear certain critics moaning over my suggestion that we befriend things. But I'm serious about this and mean it in a philosophically precise way. Throughout history, as I said, writers defining and exploring the soul wrote about friendship as the soul's signature activity. Friendship is a special kind of love that allows us to feel close to people and things in a way that is not so romantic. It rests on a deep, mutual connection as we go about our lives. Anyway, I'd rather be linked to Martha Stewart than to objectifying psychologists.

Caring for the soul of the world means first making things with an acute ethical sensitivity, making them to function well and to be beautiful, using the heart and the imagination at full throttle, and giving them as much individuality as possible. These qualities are all aspects of soul.

We might also create objects that we can relate to easily and even love. Steve Jobs, founder of Apple Computer, said, "When you're a carpenter making a beautiful chest of drawers, you're not going to use a piece of plywood on the back, even though it faces the wall and nobody will see it." You can't cheat or cut corners if you want your object to have a soul.

Once a thing is made, you don't treat it like a slave. If you're going to sell it, ask an honest price, don't trick or cheat your customer, and present it honestly. Soul requires high moral standards. Imagine if advertising presented things for our contemplation honestly and we could believe their copy and take it to heart. We'd have a better relation to things from the start. Maybe we should bring our soul-based team of therapists to Madison Avenue. I don't expect a complete conversion to marketplace morality, but any movement in that direction would be emotionally healthy for the society.

As therapists of the world, you keep things in good working order and looking good. You paint when necessary, replace parts, and keep them alive for a decent amount of time. If you really love a thing, you don't want it dying off prematurely. We also need to have old thing-friends nearby, just like old people, to give us the full range of experience.

Making by Hand

We often create a world in which things are cheap, ugly, only functional, and quick to wear out. Then we live in this kind of world and take on its qualities. A good craftsperson, a model maker of things, takes time in the making, pays attention to details, wants to make a beautiful object, and loves the things he or she makes and things that other good makers create. It's too much to expect a handcrafted world, but even machine-made things can be designed to be beautiful and suitable for human use.

The word *manufacture* means "handmade." Handmade things, in which the making is intimate enough that you bestow soul on the thing made, can be the model for all manufactured things. Keep the hand in the process, at least metaphorically and in principle.

The myth of Pygmalion as told in Ovid's *Metamorphoses* speaks to this matter with insight. The sculptor makes a beautiful woman from marble and wishes he could find a real woman like her. He makes an offering at the altar of Aphrodite. When he returns home, he kisses the stone face and feels her lips warm. In some paintings Aphrodite is shown gently placing a butterfly on the statue's head, giving it soul. This is a good image for what we could do: honor Aphrodite, the archetypal spirit of beauty and sensuality. We could welcome her back by making our things beautiful, alive, and lovable. We could easily kiss life into the objects we use.

Things in a house genuinely become members of the family. When you move, some things must move with you. If you feel pressed to part with things that have been intimately part of your life, it is right that you feel sad and find it difficult to leave them behind. That feeling of loss makes you human and shows that you and the things in your life have a soul.

You can sense the soul
In things
if you stop and look
And feel
And let the things simply be,
Revealing their past and their
Personalities.

Chapter 15

THERAPY AT WORK

Alchemists of old engaged in a process that we call "occult" but was a noble and essential lifework for them. They were hunting for a great elixir, the philosopher's stone, and the peacock's tail, all images for a refinement of natural materials by the human imagination and technical skill to make medicine and to discover the secrets of both soul and spirit. They were like astrologers as they used natural materials—chemicals and physical stuff in general—as images for the materials and workings of a human life.

Jung knew he had a treasure trove of psychology when he discovered alchemy. He did not turn a physical practice into a psychological one. One of his greatest achievements was to develop alchemical psychology, a way of going deeper into the psyche through a comprehensive set of metaphors.

"Work" on the psyche alchemists called *opus*, the Latin word for "work," to which the alchemist dedicated his life. The many experiences we all go through in a lifetime can create a soulful existence, and our deepest lifework is the Opus, the making of a realized self and a meaningful life. Our career, jobs, and vocational efforts are part of the Opus. A career and the Great Work of soul-making mirror each other.

We may think of work as a means for making a living, but it can also be the way we make sense of our lives. Our work may carry on certain skills and values of our parents and ancestors and also, metaphorically, express the path we are taking toward fulfillment. Work may also express our vision and the values we consider important. In other words, a life-work and the Opus coincide, the soul's opus rumbling in the depths of our daily work.

People often overlook the importance of work in their emotional lives and relationships. Yet the work we do is the first thing most of us think of when someone asks about us. Work and career and service have everything to do with finding meaning and purpose. It makes no sense to ignore it in therapy.

If there are problems at work, they will likely bleed over into other areas of life. I have a client who is married to a doctor. Actually, she's married to his work, because that is where he gives most of his time and attention. Work is the third party in this marriage, or, more accurately, the doctor's wife is the third factor that often interferes with his real marriage to medicine.

In your jobs and career you "work" out the raw material of your existence. You may try to complete your parents' ambitions or give your family standing. You may feel underappreciated and get praise and recognition through work. You may find fulfillment in making a contribution to society or to humanity. Changes in your work life often reflect changes in you, in who you want to be.

Soul in the Workplace

The workplace itself may be screaming with difficult emotions and relationships. Hierarchies are often a problem. Successful people often can't deal well with authority and leadership and make life difficult for those under them. Work usually creates anxiety about making enough money and keeping a job. It may either support or interfere with important relationships. A person's sense of worth and the very meaning of life often depends on what happens at work. The workplace teems with matters of soul.

Workers have to spend hours with others who are quite different from them. They may be competing for advancement, recognition, a good placement and success, vying for a higher position or just a corner office with a window. There may be erotic attractions, inappropriate friendships, and abuse of authority. In some workplaces the social climate is toxic, and the workplace itself may be in need of therapy.

Many businesses suffer from a lack of psychological understanding among leaders and workers. People can't see past the surface of relationship issues or authority problems. Therefore, many companies would benefit from some basic, ongoing education in psychological matters. Workers do their best to survive, but they don't have skills or insights that would allow them to deal with the many issues that come up. Therapy there could begin with education, learning how to detect what is going on beneath the surface of emotional problems and learning some simple ways of dealing with them. Basic psychological ideas are not so complicated and can be taught.

Today, corporate coaches help management and the workforce deal with their problems. But coaching is not exactly psychotherapy, and businesses could use more help. Emotional factors leap out in competitions for projects and for leadership roles. But they are usually unconscious, and so when emotions become intense, they become destructive. Deep coaching, a movement in the general field of coaching today, can move closer to psychotherapy, at least in the sense of soul care, helping society flourish through care for the workplace.

If I were going to help a company become more psychologically sophisticated, here are a few of the many issues I'd focus on:

1. Understand that abusive controlling leaders are usually secretly insecure and weak. If you don't perceive this contradiction, your way of dealing with them may be ineffective.

2. Jealousy and envy are to be expected in hierarchical organizations. They are raw expressions of more basic desires. You may have to be patient with these symptoms. Don't just try to get rid of them but help them ripen into more positive energies.

3. A person in authority may not deal with their position well because of bad experiences in the family and in childhood. You may need some empathic, deep discussions before you can work out solutions with them.

4. People tend to develop hostile feelings toward each other when they don't have opportunities to really get acquainted. It's too easy then to direct stray negative fantasies at fellow workers.

5. Conviviality can give the soul the security and deep satisfaction it craves. Gatherings where people can truly enjoy one another and daily breaks in a convivial atmosphere could help, not hurt, productivity.

6. Being critical and vocal about fellow workers may stem from insecurity, an overwhelming need to keep the job, or habits learned at home. A few lessons in dealing with insecurity would go a long way.

7. A business can't provide deep therapy for all its workers, but it can create a work environment that is not emotionally toxic. A sensitive style of leadership especially can help create real community, which can tone down the negativity.

8. Therapy always begins with listening. Any business could create a structure in which just listening to workers' issues could help with morale.

9. The physical environment can also soothe the soul: fresh air, plants and trees, water, a place to walk, a comfortable workstation, well-selected colors. Therapy often involves physical details; it is not just a mental activity.

10. Images affect the soul deeply. You can devote attention to the art images in the workplace or to any aspect of the place seen as an image. How do you feel in a medical center, waiting for your doctor, in a small room with no windows and perhaps plastic images of blocked arteries or diseased organs? Even a small degree of awareness

could make the image environment supportive rather than destructive.

At work, people often either are driven to succeed or feel resigned to spend their lives doing something unimportant and unengaging. People forming companies focus on financial matters or go about the process unconsciously, creating problems from the very beginning. They may overlook the basic truth about work that everyone needs meaningful and satisfying labor.

Any workplace is a human community, what the Greeks called "polis," a political group. It needs an inspiring vision, ideas, and examples. It also needs a stellar ethical sensibility, because even at work justice is a major issue. The failure of any of these will lead to psychological malaise and symptoms.

A soulful space is one in which people in it feel like human beings, have positive and constructive emotions, and experience beauty. It is not so technological and industrial that it makes the people into machines. It is a warm, human environment that is not difficult to create; you just need the imagination for it. And a humane environment would make for more productive and positive workers.

A human workspace, like all soulful endeavors, is based on the principle of friendship and so fosters friendship among workers, as well as an atmosphere of friendliness, an important cousin to friendship. Friendship is one of the main signs that soul is present, and yet some business owners and managers worry that friendship will slow production. Many workers feel inspired to do their work well because of the friends they have on the job.

A Lifework

It helps to distinguish between a job and a lifework. The latter is whatever is done in the course of a lifetime to make you feel that you have made a contribution and your life has been worthwhile. A career is part of that lifework, but so are avocations and service done for your community.

In my book *Ageless Soul* I told the story of a man who had been a lawyer in his career, but in retirement he helped young classical musicians develop a program performing in people's homes. He spoke of this "retirement" career as giving him profound satisfaction and sense of meaning. This is not to say that his life as a lawyer was not fulfilling and essential but that the retirement "job" touched his heart and engaged his love of art and young people. His experience is a good model for anyone in search of lifelong meaningful work.

When you consider your lifework, which is an important consideration, you have to look beyond your career, even if your job makes up the bulk of it. Service in particular can give you the feeling that your life is valuable and that your time has been well spent. You give others your time and energy, and you get back a sense of real accomplishment.

The Great Work

In therapeutic conversations, therefore, I listen for the deeper and often hidden lifework that is being lived out by means of the surface jobs and side activities. I wonder what action this person is "called to." I don't mean anything supernatural or naïvely spiritual. Most of us feel that we have a purpose in life, and one hopes that a career fulfills that purpose. Does it have the deep meaning I need? Does it take me along the path to my own fulfillment? Does it allow me to make a contribution to humanity, however small, and therefore give my life some dignity?

Anyone spending time at a job that is meaningless is going to feel lost. How can you be engaged in life if your job drains your soul? The therapist's task is to help find ways to nourish the soul, to keep it healthy and strong, a fertile and supportive base for all that you do. So in therapy it is worth talking about your work. Maybe with a deeper vision you can make adjustments to your work life as a way of solving what seem to be unrelated problems and making the whole of life more satisfying.

A therapist could help workers explore their experience of jobs and careers. "Have they corresponded to your nature and character?" "Have they expressed your values?" "Have you been brought closer to your vision of what you want the world to be?" "Do you feel good about these jobs, or do you have regrets?" Your work experience does not have to be perfect, and even bad decisions and choices have a place in your life story.

Often care of the soul takes place in the guise of conversations about technical issues at work or personal matters that would appear to be about workplace social dynamics. Yet a little probing may reveal that the issue is deeply personal or transferred from home to the workplace. Managers at all levels may find themselves dealing with emotional issues beyond their power to heal. Still, they can offer care that may improve the situation without necessarily solving the deeper problem.

I would offer them a checklist:

1. Listen closely.
2. Give advice cautiously.
3. Feed back what you hear at a deeper level.
4. Affirm the person.
5. Help deepen the story.

With these simple actions you are calling up the therapist in you. You can accomplish a great deal with these few steps. You may be surprised at the magic that happens when you listen closely and feed back what you hear, not just literally but the tone and the telling details. When you get to the point of doing these five steps well and smoothly, you can consider yourself a fledgling therapist. Of course you don't want to confuse this capacity with professional therapy, but you can offer your care and help with some sophistication and intelligence.

It would make sense to have a professional therapist visit a company and teach managers and maybe all employees how to talk to each other effectively. It is not only true that some things have to be taught but also that many things we assume don't have to be taught do. We need some instruction on how to speak to each other in ways that help rather than hurt. We are all capable of being useful to another person, especially when they are in distress. To help a friend, coworker, or family member, you can keep it simple. It takes a cool and subtle intelligence to speak both simply and effectively. You have to learn how to listen and how to use words.

The Power of Words

Talking therapeutically at the workplace may be complicated by social hierarchies and rules and matters of privacy. But often certain people in an organization are asked to help with behavior issues, absenteeism, and emotional difficulties on the job. Managers especially may have to be temporary therapists, whether they want to or not. It would be in their interest to learn how to listen and to talk in ways that are at least useful and potentially healing.

The workplace is an especially good place for therapeutic discussion. Many challenging issues are floating in the air. There is a sense of immediacy. You don't have to play at being a therapist; you only have to take ordinary conversations a step or two deeper. If you recognize an important issue in the conversation, don't let it go by. Be the one who makes conversation real, and you are the appointed therapist of the moment.

If you are a psychotherapist working with an organization, you can apply all the recommendations of this book, understanding that a group is made up of individuals, each with their own psychological issues, and that a group has its own psychology, as well: its history and problematical tendencies. As always, these need a hearing and insight. It's probably better if you're not a genius at analysis but rather understand therapy primarily as a work of the heart. People in organizations usually have little heart satisfaction and therefore suffer the special heart ailments of the psyche.

At the workplace people also need spiritual inspiration and vision. It does not take much to place their work in the context of a lifework or a contribution to humanity. The trouble with most work is that it is too narrowly focused and could use an expanded vision. It may also be contributing more to greed and self-interest than to the human community, and that ethical limitation has an impact on how workers see their jobs. A therapist can do many things to make work a true reflection of the soul's opus.

As an author traveling often on book tours, I found myself speaking to different groups of workers—hospitals, booksellers, chamber musicians, spa owners, and at Starbucks headquarters. I found that by delving deeper into the products and services these people offered, I could give them a vision that would inspire them in their work. I was surprised how simple it was to give new meaning to ordinary work. It showed me how small a vision most people have of their lifework, and how depressing that kind of work can be. It would not take much to bring soul to our society simply by being reminded of the importance of our work.

A job or piece of labor
Is always an initiation of the soul
In which you discover eternal truths
With your hands and eyes
And making is a hint of the purpose
Of your life.

Chapter 16

HEALING SOCIETY'S SOUL

A society is like a person. It has a special history, certain inclinations, fears, hopes, and habits. A culture can get depressed and harbor old angers. A society has a personal history that needs sorting and clearing out, and it can always use some good therapy.

Psychotherapists who spend their time listening closely to people's emotional difficulties and life battles learn a great deal about human experience, and therefore they have much to offer society at large. They can write, make films, and give interviews that benefit their communities. But ordinary people, too, can become therapists for their society. They can become involved in the greater life around them and bring their sensitive perspective to problems. They can be caring rather than argumentative and offer therapeutic wisdom where it is needed.

Therapists could imagine politics that care for society

rather than the politician or party. Of course, politicians give lip service to this ideal, but there is no reason, except for cynicism and failure of imagination, why it couldn't be put into practice. The politician needs some education and guided reflection on the job, imagining it as therapeutic by nature. One of my purposes here is to give the role of therapist high stature so we all, at appropriate times, could take it on.

Practicing Therapy in the World

Therapy does not have to take the form of conversation. It may involve painting a house, building good transportation, inviting fresh and useful businesses to a region. In the little New England town where I live there is a small group of businesspeople who are concerned about the future of the region and do everything they can to provide attractive buildings and a good economy for all. They work hard to keep the international chain stores at a distance from the town center, so that they don't quash local initiatives. They bury cables and raise money for improvements. They keep up the beautiful old buildings and demand strict codes for new ones. They are the town's therapists, and they take their calling seriously.

I talk to these people, who have skills that I lack. I encourage them and try to give them some philosophical underpinning for their good work. I'm their therapist. Therapists always need therapists.

As part of my work I often speak to radio hosts who discuss topics on air that are of interest and useful to their listeners. They are therapists, offering opportunities for thoughtful conversations. The listeners hear ideas that may help them sort out their lives and arrange their values. In my experience the station and format matter little. I often talk about the soul between sports and the weather, and very often these AM-radio hosts are bright and full of heart.

In our town we have an old-fashioned family-run small market. Conversations are going on everywhere in this store, and people refer to one another by name. Many who work there have been employed at this store for many years, one older man since his teens. A friendly woman runs the register, and we talk about her trips to Florida in the winter. She tells me how to take care of myself and my family. This is therapy.

To appreciate what I'm saying here, you have to look past the surface. My care for my wife may lie at the heart of that conversation at the store about Florida. My marriage is involved and my deepest emotions and the very meaning of my life. I may leave the store with a few words echoing in me, feeling hope that I did not have when I entered. Nothing is as obvious or as shallow as it appears to be. I could discuss the issues with a professional therapist, but he may not be as "therapeutic" as the store clerk.

Other important therapists of the culture are dentists, doctors, nurses, and physical therapists. Over the years I have had many conversations in hospitals about the importance of the receptionists, who are the first contact with patients.

If they present a caring attitude, you enter the process of healing well prepared. If they are abrupt or impatient, which is sometimes the case, you will begin your process of healing on a negative note.

Doctors often mistakenly see their job as a technical one and don't realize how important it might be for them to treat their patients as human beings instead of a collection of organs. These days some stare at their laptops and don't look at their patients. It's rare for a doctor to use a patient's ordinary name. When I go to a doctor, I keep repeating, "My name's Tom," yet the doctor rarely uses my name.

I've heard of psychotherapists, too, who keep their noses in their laptops as their clients spill out difficult confessions and worries. I wish I could send them an old, yellowing copy of one of Carl Rogers's basic books. Haven't we learned yet in medicine and psychology that the person counts and deserves our full attention?

Any project loses its soul when the people at the top exploit the process for their own gain, whether financial or egotistical. But a community of people focused around common concerns, the polis, is made up of individuals, and it is not easy to reach anything close to consensus. Especially in politics, people are forever getting caught in complexes, working out their parental transferences with political leaders and fighting over the homeland.

Emotional transference goes on in government and politics. When people gather together to follow a leader, male or female, they are in a position similar to the one they knew as a child: the mother and father were powerful, mythlike figures playing a dominant role in their psyches. Elements in this pattern crop up in political groups, where the leader serves as a mother or father. I don't mean that they stand in for personal parents, although that may be the case sometimes, but that the archetypal father and mother have big roles in politics. Many people, indeed maybe most of us, are always looking for a mother and father to comfort and direct the child of the psyche. We may find one in the political scene and quickly devote ourselves to a politician's leadership. Barack Obama quickly evoked this pattern in millions of people around the globe when he first appeared on the scene. Others saw something vile and destructive in him, perhaps because of his rather liberal views, his race, or his hope to restore civility. Some polarization is part of politics, but when it is extreme, it requires therapy, and as in most therapies, solutions are not easy to find.

One way is for each citizen to tame the tendency within them to polarize. This is a form of self-therapy, knowing that you have a neurotic habit of vilifying your opponent and wanting to find another way. Leaders can be effective, too, by encouraging their followers not to polarize. In that case, political leaders activate the therapist in their followers.

Professional psychotherapists could play an influential role in the polis. They know human nature better than anyone, and they have much to offer. Their simple comments on destructive interactions could educate the public toward more civil and effective discourse.

Social Unconsciousness

The root problem in society is an astounding degree of unconsciousness in dealings among people. Many act and speak from their deep needs, long-standing neurotic patterns and fears—with little or no awareness. You see this in shouting matches in which people hear nothing of what the other has to say. A community thrives on a spirit of cooperation and empathy, but often what you see is pure narcissism, self-interest, and gross immaturity.

Education and therapy usually go together, but our people have almost no education in how to be citizens: how to listen, really converse, value consensus, appreciate diversity, understand the importance of exchanging ideas. Most don't know the difference between an opinion and an idea. Few aspire to the Greek ideal of *aretē*, or excellence of character.

One obvious solution would be to teach the psychology of self-government, raising awareness about what it takes to sustain a well-functioning society. This teaching could be done in high school and in more public arenas for adults. But how many people even think about the psychological issues in voting, debating, and meeting to solve social problems? We need a revolution in how society thinks of itself, a means of becoming more mature and thoughtful about social interaction. We need communal therapy, and we need it urgently.

We are back at Rule Number One: some things have to be taught. You can't expect an average person to know the rules of effective engagement with others. Usually people are only aware of their own needs and values that have come from their unconscious families and that have never been questioned or matured. Rule Number Two: some things have to be healed. When people gather, there are many emotional wounds caught up in the discussion of social issues. You can see the pain on people's faces as they desperately argue on behalf of their own needs and beliefs. It's difficult to sustain a creative and happy society when the need for therapy is so strong and when little therapy is being offered.

A person who has been in therapy, even if it has only been accidental therapy, helpful intimate discussion with friends, understands the difference between raw emotions and thoughtful feelings. Therapy can indeed work, not only at solving problems but in creating a style of behavior that involves less acting out and more self-awareness. Imagine a society in which the citizens have reached a level of self-possession and sophistication allowing them to entertain a variety of viewpoints in a context of cultural diversity.

Martin Luther King Jr. was a therapist for American society. He pointed out our blindness and offered suggestions for increased awareness. His role and purpose was not only to liberate Black people but to free all citizens from emotional blockage to community. In his stirring and famous "I Have a Dream" speech, he said: "Let us not seek to satisfy our thirst for freedom by drinking from the cup of bitterness and hatred. . . . Again and again we must rise to the majestic heights of meeting physical force with soul force." That "soul force" is the power of psyche, and Dr. King was doing soul therapy.

Politicians and government leaders are meant to be therapists for society. It's their job. Usually they don't understand this and can't find the distance from their parties and positions to speak therapeutically. Once in a while you see remarkable exceptions. Citizens, too, can be therapists, if only they can rise above the passions of their tribe and speak to the needs of the entire community. Conversely, professional therapists are citizens, and they could be as involved with their society as with their individual clients.

> Society is a very large man or woman
> With all the neuroses that come with
> Manhood and womanhood
> And with all the potential for
> Love and good and beauty
> That we smaller men and women
> Are capable of.

Chapter 17

PARENTS AS SOUL GUIDES

When I was in my teens, at the end of each summer I would leave home and go back to the seminary boarding school in a distant city to continue my march toward the Catholic priesthood. A strong vision was guiding my life, but emotionally it was difficult to leave my warm and supportive family. One of those times, my aunt pulled me aside and said, "Tommy, if you ever feel that it's time to leave that life and come home, don't hesitate. We will all understand and welcome you back."

That was an important moment for me that I have never forgotten. I am always grateful to my aunt for saying those therapeutic words to me. I'm sure they helped when it was the day of decision and I did come home and was concerned about disappointing my family.

She was not giving me advice or telling me what I should do. She was making me feel accepted and loved no matter which way my life went. She was speaking for the family and knew that my parents would feel the same. She was acting as a momentary therapist, saying just the right caring words.

Care of a Child's Soul

All parents—aunts and uncles, too—are called to be caretakers of the soul, the souls of the children. Children see events through hypersensitive eyes and have their own magnified impressions about the world. They often explode in joy, but their happiness offsets deep fears and dreads. Their pain can be so devastating as to upset their very souls. In this bigger-than-life arena, parents are figures of myth, literally. Wounds to the child's soul can be immeasurably deep and may last a lifetime.

We live in a machine age, the era of the computer and other wonderful gadgets. Without thinking about it, we transfer that mechanical thinking to children and want to fill them with knowledge and technical skills. We hope they learn science and math and have enough technical knowledge to make a good living. We don't give nearly as much attention to the soul subjects like art and literature, and we don't even think about supporting the child as his or her soul gradually comes into view. Education as care of the child's soul seems out of step with the times, but it would not take much to reverse this trend, just a shift in the way we imagine life.

The care of a child's soul requires restraint and close observation. You have to see how the child finds ways to allow her essence to manifest. A parent's job as soul educator is to "lead out" the child's soul into actual life, and this will give rise to a unique individual. *Educere*, one Latin root of education, means "to lead out." The other, *educare*, means "to raise and teach." If you're really doing education, you don't put things into the child, you lead out what is already there and is uniquely the child's. You can't expect the child to be like other children or indeed like you.

The great challenge of parents is to find it in themselves to support the emergence of a new original person. Education and emergence are two sides of the coin by which a child makes an appearance. The soul has its own seed nature and its own ways. It is the spring from which individuality surfaces, and so to care for a child's soul is to prize the unexpected ways that person comes into view. *Emergence*, which means "coming out after being submerged," should be a key word in a child's education.

As a child, I was told to be submerged, not to show myself, not to speak up, not to appear. This was the opposite of education as leading out. I know from my work as a therapist that many were raised as I was to stay submerged. Somehow we emerge anyway, probably because we have a stream of parents and teachers our whole life long, people who are pleased to father and mother us, many of whom want to see us emerge.

Love and acceptance fill the atmosphere of a soul-oriented home. You don't have to push your child to do anything but only trust the seed of a self that you glimpse. Over time it will unfold into a creative individual—if you don't interfere. A parent has to be a trusting person, supporting the child even in the face of awkward attempts to be an individual in an environment that delights in conformity. People like children to behave well, which means to conform and comply (Winnicott, 1971, p. 65). Children naturally want to be themselves.

A therapist is often called upon to be a great parent for his client—mother, father, or both. This is the deepest and most positive countertransference, to accept the role of parent and do it without ego and self-serving and unconsciousness. To be willing to a person's parent, to stand in where others have been lacking.

If you wish to grasp a particular child's soul for care, notice what he or she fears or finds joy in. Individual sensitivity is a key sign of soul. Look at the people she befriends, since friendship is a key element in a soulful life. What does he do when he plays? Play is like dreaming, a world within a world that the soul likes to inhabit or visit. Surely, you will see signs of a future career or lifestyle in a young child. You can nurture that seedling without pressure or demand. The soul does not respond well to force. It wants room to expand and blossom, and it needs understanding and support.

The Parent's Child

A parent fosters the child's soul by modeling a life of self-trust and deep caring. For most parents that means dealing with wounds from their own childhood, instead of working them out at the child's expense. Just a little psychological insight could prevent a great deal of suffering: know this simple principle, parents—you may try to correct your own childhood issues by acting them out with your children. With a little insight, you can spot this pattern and avoid it, giving your child a chance.

Therapists know, and I know, how sad it is to talk with adults who have many stories to tell of parents who got angry at them regularly, suppressed their spirit, and wounded them seriously—all due to a parent's ignorance about the basic psychology of raising children. I repeat the fundamental principle: let the genius in the child emerge roughly at first and then mature into adult character. Be patient and loving. That is all that is necessary.

If you find yourself getting angry at your child and demanding that she obey you and be the person you expect her to be, find some therapy in which you can work out your own childhood issues. As you begin your role as parent, that is a perfect time to revisit your childhood and work through your own confusion and pain.

Professional therapists learn the same lesson. If they want to help their clients deal with emotional difficulties, they themselves should be in therapy during their training, so that they might be less likely to act out their past issues with their clients. This acting out on the part of both professionals and parents can be subtle. When you are directing your pain and frustration toward your child, you may feel justified, because momentarily you see the child as a proper object of your anger. You think you're doing it with your child's best interests in mind. But you are transferring your emotions from a past experience to a present one, from people you should be angry at to a child who is simply at hand and an easy target. Your thought that your anger is good for the child is an illusion or a way of justifying your understandable but misplaced rage.

A parent can relate to children therapeutically, in the sense developed in this book, by listening closely to what the child has to say and trying to hear the deeper message. A child may speak in terms that are not as clear and direct as an adult. Children try to convey their experience and their feelings, but they simply are not old enough. A parent listens for the real message with care and patience. A remarkable parent catches the metaphors and underlying messages in a child's statements and behavior.

A good therapist relates in confident adult fashion to the child soul in his client. He notices where a parent has been lacking, and fills in. He reconnects with the child in his own soul and remembers the wounds he suffered as a child. He develops empathy with the child of memory appearing now in the sometimes painful tales of childhood.

Separation Happens

One message that a parent might easily overlook or misread is the child's need, at times, to begin the separation from family into adult independence. It may start early with slight efforts to be different and maybe even disobey. D. W. Winnicott, the celebrated child psychoanalyst, said that with children you have a choice. You can expect them to play with you or to be compliant. To be compliant is to slowly die to the self. Yet parents often demand compliance. "You should do it because I said so." "Children should obey their parents." Just a little reflection would reveal the egotism and desperation in these sentences used every day with children.

Parents, children have to separate from you and eventually live their own lives. Deep down, you may be sad and angry about this fact of life. But your job is to help your child pull away from you and be a distinct, independent person. To be successful at this, children may have to practice it from early childhood. You have to see through their outbursts to the drama being played out. They are not disobeying you personally, they are freeing themselves from the archetypal mother and father. Believe it or not, you are not the object of their anger, even if they think so and lead you to believe it. They need to be free of any form of overbearing and limited version of Father and Mother. They need to grow up and ease out of the family circle and move into a larger world where they will find new avatars for the archetypal parents.

If you can be therapeutic rather than reactively personal, you can help the child mature. Yes, it takes some stamina from you, but that's a small price for the deep satisfaction of being an effective parent. Besides, the situation could help you grow up, too, so you won't be expecting others to obey you and honor your every word. You, too, need to be free of the weighty archetypes of Father and Mother. You need to grow out and escape from a limited, heavy, suffocating role.

A parent can check with the child to be sure he's getting the right message. The Rogersian client-centered approach becomes a child-centered approach. Listening, linked to positive regard, is the key. In this case positive regard means being on the child's side, understanding that behavior is usually symbolic. In actions that may annoy the parent, the child is trying to express displeasure or pain or trying to separate. The child may speak and behave indirectly, so the parent has to have some skill at reading words and actions metaphorically. Never take anything at face value. Always expect nuances, indirect messages, and a considerable amount of symbolism. Remember, the child is separating from the Great Mother and the Great Father, not from you.

A child has reason to be afraid of a parent who is bigger than she is, has more power and authority, safeguards the child with a home and financial support, and has a storehouse of love that the child needs. A parent must have a therapist in her to help the child deal with life issues that face a child several times a day. It is not easy being a child: small dramas feel huge, one incapacity or another is always getting in the way, and it is not easy to understand the complex matters unfolding all around.

Parent as Tennis Pro

As a therapist, the parent speaks and responds—not reacts—like a tennis pro, as I said before. It is not natural. You don't just whack the ball. You think about what you're doing and use proper form. You use words that don't just smack your kid with power but meet at the proper angle and technique. You hit the ball so she can hit it back and enjoy the game and feel like a pro.

You want to promote confidence, awareness, and skill. And so you have to be skillful, patient, and thoughtful. This is how a good therapist talks. He does not say everything that comes into his mind. He's honest and present but always uses words carefully, aware of their potential impact and how they will or won't coincide with his aim at making his client feel strong and able. The therapist parent builds a vessel in which the child can feel free to be herself, like nowhere else on earth.

I sometimes dream of becoming a professor
At the University of Parenthood.
Here men and women take classes
In Play, Life Lessons, and Hurt Feelings.
They get their diplomas and are then ready
To spoon and nuzzle and bring a new soul
Into a waiting world.

Part 5

THE THERAPIST

Socrates was profoundly convinced that man's moral existence harmonizes with the natural order of the world. . . . What is new in his thought is his belief that man cannot reach this harmony with Being through the cultivation and satisfaction of his own senses and his bodily nature, but only through complete mastery over himself in accordance with the law he finds by searching his own soul.

—*Werner Jaeger (1943, p. 45)*

A psychotherapist and a helping friend play an important role in allowing people to get through the difficulties that inevitably come up in an ordinary life. But the work requires a high degree of self-possession. Psychotherapy is an art rooted in skills and personal character.

Chapter 18

COUPLES IN THERAPY

When two people meet and fall in love, they enter a state like no other. Emotions are high. Their fantasies center on being together forever, and often for a long time they can't stop thinking about each other. Other values, like work and education, may fall to the overwhelming power of the new love. This state is so intense and special that to call it love may mislead the victims. It is not so much that they love, as you might love a child or a parent, but that they have become electrified by their passion and blinded by their illusions. A cloud of strong emotion and delirious fantasy engulfs them.

The "love" in "falling in love" sometimes proves to be a huge inflation, so that when the exalted fantasies diminish, the people involved feel *disillusioned*. That's a good word, because indeed they have lost their delicious illusion that was perhaps sweeter than the possibility of a real relationship. But I don't use the word *illusion* negatively. We need our passing spells and visits to wonderland. They may put us to sleep at one level, but at another they take us into new possibilities and keep us there, charmed, until new life can take hold.

Jung says that when love like this is unconscious, there can be no real relationship. You have to have some awareness outside the bubble of romantic love to truly relate. This description makes a good deal of sense, but I would also turn it upside down. We need the dream state of love to take us out of our habits and lethargy. It is not the final step in a relationship evolving, but it is a crucial one. I imagine romantic love as a glowing aura of fairy-tale wishes with the seed of real love at its core.

Ecstasy has an important place in a human life. If all we do is cruise along every day in an alert, rational condition, life becomes flat, predictable, and too controlled. In the introduction to my book *The Re-Enchantment of Everyday Life*, I wrote this sentence that still makes sense to me: "The soul has an absolute, unforgiving need for regular excursions into enchantment. It requires them like the body needs food and the mind needs thought" (Moore, 1996, p. ix).

Leaving rationality for the deep and lively imagination of the soul does far more than offer relief from habitual consciousness. In that realm is our future. It is where we find inspiration and a great vision. It shakes us up emotionally, gives us a push, and fills us with new desires, an essential condition of the soul.

Romantic love is one of the strongest enticements out of old habits we will ever experience. Jung warned us about its dangers, and Hillman celebrated its capacity to bring the soul to life. A therapist could protect the enchantment as well as the conscious union of a couple, rather than moralistically remind them of the dangers. The enchantment of love can persist for years if it is fostered and cultivated. Later it may not be as strong as it once was, but a little of its magic goes a long way.

Jung went to pains to articulate the kind of positioning in life you need to be open to both the imagination and having a strong direction. For instance, he used the word *Self* in a special way, meaning a firm consciousness and ego sense plus a regular opening to the Unconscious, as he would put it—I would say soul and the deep imagination. He wrote about the "transcendent function," an appreciation for images that serve awareness and yet reside in part in that realm of deep imagination. In the case of romantic love, you need both consciousness and the willingness to be lost in illusion. It does not have to be either-or.

Normally we don't consider the "mania," as Plato called it, of love sufficiently dangerous to require therapy. But any escapes from reality would benefit from a degree of self-awareness. The love state is not a good place for making decisions. This kind of love fogs the mind and inspires irrational behavior. When it turns dark, especially, as in serious jealousy, it can be truly dangerous.

Being swept up in love is one of the beautiful aspects of human life, but working out the relationship in real life can be less inspiring. Therapists often meet a couple after the warm and exciting illusion has settled and they are facing the practicalities of real life, to say nothing of the partner suddenly emerging out of the mist of illusion. A therapist needs to feel at home in both realms, the sane and the illusional, without favoring the sane, and deal effectively with the emotional area where they overlap.

Therapists are often on the side of rationality and see illusion as the enemy. That is why we need a "Romantic Movement" in the field of psychology, an appreciation for what the poet John Donne called "the extasie of love":

> Our soules, (which to advance their state,
> Were gone out,) hung 'twixt her, and mee.

Notice Donne's words, "to advance their state, Were gone out." That is Hillman's point: the illusions of love advance the soul, even if that state can cause trouble. Incidentally, Donne's poems on love contain insights into the psychology of love that a psychotherapist today might consider modern.

Romantic love is a serious illusion because it can mark the most significant turning point in your life. The movement toward coupling, being married or at least long-term partners, having children, and establishing a family serve one of the deepest structures of your life. So you allow the dreamstate of love to linger as it takes you from one condition in life to another. This love is like a mist-covered bridge taking you blindly (remember how Cupid, the angel of love, is portrayed with a band around his eyes) to your next major phase. If the love does not result in a new serious coupling, it could be a step in that direction.

The Community Around Lovers

When you unite in love, you are bringing with you your family history, your wounds and expectations, and probably your past experiences of love. You may even be carrying the confusion of a divorce or separation. The past is always present. In fact, this new love may excite old experiences and make them even more of an issue.

During the full assault of love we owe a great deal to friends who may challenge and comfort us. They can see how foolish we are with our now ecstasies, now broken hearts, and yet they respond seriously. Everyone knows that love can make you foolish, and for the most part people accept it. No one goes to a psychiatrist simply because they have fallen in love.

Still, there is need for some words of support and clarification. To expand on Plato, he said that love is one thing that can cause us to lose our mind creatively and positively. Erotic madness he called it, after Eros, the god of romantic love, the god who later became Cupid as our estimation of love's power shrank. *Mania* was Plato's word for madness, and it makes sense that such a mania could use a therapist's understanding ear. It was the same Plato who defined therapy as care and service.

I consider my approach to the therapy of love basically Platonic. I see this kind of love as having its own beauty and value, for all its illusions and potential disaster. Like Plato, I understand it as an expression of the soul, the soul coming out of its protective shell to move life onward. The madness of love is only the start. It may lead to a successful relationship and to creative work, to children and a greater life. If instead it leads to bitter separation, that, too, in a darker manner can serve the soul.

From a Jungian perspective, the experience of love brings to life certain central unconscious complexes that show up as infatuation and compulsion. Love takes on highly neurotic aspects that need reflection and consideration—therapy. The benefit of the classical Jungian approach is that we stop talking literally about the actual people involved and consider the inner persons, the hidden life that has erupted in romance.

When couples get together, at first they don't know what is happening to them. They talk to each other as much as possible to find out who that other person is. They may get married while still in the cloud of romance, so that, as so many people say, they wake up later and discover that while largely unconscious they have made a major life decision. They are now linked to a person who is no longer quite so wrapped in a wonder-filled cloud. For many, marriage involves an almost daily quest to discover just who this person is they have married.

Most couples manage to keep some of the romance as they develop a more realistic connection to their spouse. Fortunately, some illusions can sustain attacks from reality and can give soul to day-to-day loving. Some couples are simply *disillusioned*—that key word—and discover the crucible of relationship. There is a contradiction here: we worry about the illusions of love, but then we behold the disastrous effects of being disillusioned.

The psyche has an odd but common tendency to act out negative emotions that arose with people in the past with current friends and lovers. So, as the illusion dissipates, strong, freewheeling emotions may arise and be directed at the convenient person who is largely a stranger. The drifting away of illusions leaves behind an intimate roommate but an unknown partner.

My own view is that marriage is a vessel in which we can explore life with a companion. Happiness is not the goal as much as vitality, to be saved from a dull existence. This is not the ordinary wish to have a perfect life—a luxurious home, a good job, and successful children—but a profound and essential urge from the very root of our being to become somebody. At the wedding, most people don't know what they are looking for. Their emotions have a great deal of energy but not much content or direction. It often takes time for a marriage to gel into a form that supports both people in their movement toward meaning.

How a therapist pictures marriage and intimate partnerships shapes his approach. If he sees it as a vessel of exploration instead of the fusion of two people like molten metal, he will not be surprised at conflict and painful periods. He will be able to help the couple stay in the vessel and discover the kind of love that lasts. Instead of seeing the many ups and downs and offshoots and byways of the relationship as aberrations and threats, he will appreciate them as natural elements in the process of establishing intimacy. He will recognize that a couple is made of two individuals who do not surrender their individuality when they couple.

A relationship is a living thing. It goes through many changes, threats, joys, accomplishments, and defeats. If the couple can tolerate vitality, the relationship will have a future. Otherwise it will fade away. A therapist can give the people a vision that will sustain them through many changes. He can also help them keep the in-love feeling, because reality does not get rid of it entirely. Another way of putting it is that he can assist them as they shift from a destructive narrative into a positive one. He can also help them sort out what they are going through and see more deeply into the maturing of their love. Insight is essential and can effect change.

Think of people living together as woven together. They are facing life as single people, but as a fabric with many strands, beginning with two family and cultural backgrounds, and probably many other kinds, as well. They have to work out the complexity between themselves but then they deal with the world with the added strength of a team. Their differences can be their strengths, and if a therapist could see this potential, he might be better able to clarify the problems that arise. They may not have to get rid of the problems but rather see the positive possibilities in them.

Adolf Guggenbühl-Craig (1977) saw this long, intimate connectedness as a form of individuation, becoming a soulful person and couple: "This life-long dialectical encounter between two partners, the bond of man and woman until death [the bond of two people], can be understood as a special path for discovering the soul, as a special form of individuation" (p. 41).

Parents at the Wedding

Our fantasies constantly refer back to childhood and the early experience of our parents' adult life. Since no families are perfect, we always bring some wounding to our relationships. It might be subtle, like a mother's overprotectiveness, or outrageous, like an uncle's abuse. We make a mistake wanting each other to be perfect. The couple would have a better chance if they could understand the paradox that imperfect people relate better than perfect ones.

Remember that a person's memory of a parent is always both personal and archetypal. Every relationship needs a good Great Mother and Great Father. Somehow the people involved have to evoke a parental spirit in the relationship. They need soothing for their emotional wounds and direction for living out a relationship that started out in a romantic bubble. They have to be patient with each other and offer both strength and nurturance. Even a romantic relationship can be a form of therapy, one partner caring deeply for the other.

Parents are always major players in the personal mythology. In my experience, in therapy it's always useful to tell the stories of the parents in great detail and repeat those stories until the many illusions and denials fade into accurate portraits. The point is not to understand exactly how the parents affected the child but which archetypal figures were elicited. What was the narrative? What were the characters like?

Neutrality, Neutrality

You are the therapist, but you also become the third party in the relationship. The couple will talk about you and be aware of your positions and your presence. You are the third factor that may be able to break up the dyad that is too tight and fixed. Your neutrality is a new factor in the relationship and can have a positive impact simply by being there.

Through your focus on the soul rather than behavior, you intensify your position as a third and neutral factor. When

I have done couples therapy in the past, on occasion I asked one partner to sit in a chair off to the side while I worked with the dreams and life stories of the other. My idea was that the people did not really know each other. Maybe by listening to each other and exploring their psyches they might have more empathy and a deeper appreciation for what the other was dealing with.

As couples share their lives, they may come to think that they really know the other well. But that kind of intimacy can be misleading. Familiarity is not knowledge, and, in fact, it may be a block to really knowing the partner as a separate person. Some distance is necessary, hence my practice of attending to one person at a time. I encourage the one partner to be a close observer, perhaps gaining some empathy for the other.

By listening to the soul I mean hearing the story that can't be told. It may be too painful and disturbing, but it shows glimpses of itself now and then. You might also listen for the longings that lie deep within the other person, or their fears. You listen for the things that the other partner himself is not aware of. You hope to glimpse her essence, what she is made of at the most basic level. Hillman often said, "What does the soul want?" That is always a useful question, especially when you find the situation overwhelmingly complicated or emotional.

Honor the Shadow in a Relationship

It also helps to remember that relationships are vessels for developments in the soul and the setting of the alchemy through which a person or a couple discover their souls. In that alchemy are to be found dark elements, challenges, and even apparent impossibilities. But the struggle to become a person and to have a genuine relationship can hold people together, perhaps more effectively than a desire for happiness and unbroken togetherness. I'm not saying that a relationship should be painful but that the happiness sought for might be deep and complex, not superficial and simplistic.

Therapists who aim at simple happiness for a couple in their care may either feel frustrated eventually or misguide the couple toward an ideal of superficial togetherness. Instead, you might seek an alternative to romantic fusion or a facade of happiness. You also have to watch out for the suppression of conflict and shadow that may only create deeper and more emotional dissatisfaction.

There is a kind of happiness in a relationship that does not require constant peace. Disagreements and frustrations don't have to negate happiness but can give it the shadow necessary to be real and lasting. If a therapist feels she has to help the couple create constant calm, she may be contributing to the problem. She needs a philosophy of relationship that is suitably complicated and cognizant of the shadow.

The Too-Big Therapist

In matters of relationship, therapists have to be especially aware of their own past and present experiences and keep their own struggles separate from the couple they are trying to help. Relationship is not only a vessel for soul work; for many people it is the hottest and most active arena in which the soul works out its values and its destiny. Its themes and high energy can be contagious, and a therapist is always susceptible.

It takes courage and a high degree of self-possession to help other people sort out their relationships. It would be easy for a therapist to find himself at work on his own issues through the material presented by his clients. Also, if you take a client's statements literally, you will miss the underlying matters that press so heavily on the couple. You always have to listen between the sentences and catch the metaphors, the hidden meanings, and the evasions.

It may not be necessary to make an absolute distinction between a therapist's own struggles and those of the people he is caring for. It may be possible to take a troublesome case as the opportunity to go deeper into her own issues. But unconsciously to confuse one for the other might unravel the therapy. I believe that I have done some of my best therapy at times when my own relationships were painful and struggling, but I also know that at times I got caught and led my client in the wrong direction because of my relationship biases.

I felt raw and imperfect at those times, and the resulting vulnerability helped me do the work. But in the early years of my practice I was going through big changes, and I know that at times I was blind to the other person's different issues. I felt humbled by my own difficulties and therefore dealt with clients with considerable empathy. But, looking back, I can see that my own pain influenced me too much in certain directions. Once my own life settled down, my work as a therapist improved. I did not lose empathy, and I felt a better distance between my own life and my client's.

The key in working with couples is to have immense compassion for their struggles but also a strong sense for how relationships work and how the deep soul is involved. It may be important not to accept the stories and points of view presented in therapy but to be always on the alert for alternative explanations. Almost always, after a long and passionate tale of woe and desperation, full of explanations and the assignment of blame, I offer an alternative point of view.

Dealing with couples you have to keep in mind the soul of the relationship and not just the souls of the persons. Where is the relationship headed? What does it want? What are its complaints as distinct from the concerns of the two individuals? Couples therapy is mainly about psyche and eros swirling around in the stimulated atmosphere of the couple.

> The Great Goddess makes animals couple
> Giving her deep pleasure,
> Hinting that all our coupling is animal
> From a place where the body and strong feelings lead,
> Hinting that coupling is divinely inspired
> And should be treated with unlimited respect
> As the most perfect way to be human.

Chapter 19

A THERAPIST'S SELF-CARE

The main tool in therapy is the person of the therapist. You have to boldly enter the emotional field of a troubled person or a conflicted couple and use everything you have to help them sort out their lives. Ideas and techniques help, but they are for the most part in the background. The therapist has to use himself, at some risk, to care for the other's suffering. If anyone needs care of his own soul, it is a therapist.

This is also true of the informal "therapist," the friend counseling a friend, a coworker helping another make a big decision. Being a temporary adviser is not your career, but for the moment you do need to take care of yourself. Give of your energy and time only as much as you can afford. Know your limits. Give yourself rest and pleasures that can both calm and invigorate you for this special, taxing work.

A therapist's job is demanding. Every human life is infinitely complex, and motives are deep, subtle, and hard to perceive. The past keeps worming in to upset the present, and it's difficult and time-consuming to sort it all out. Emotions are high, and sometimes they're directed toward the therapist. Threats of lawsuit are a possibility, and there is no final outcome. There is pressure from the profession to stay up-to-date and follow guidelines. Life goes on.

A therapist needs not only usual forms of relaxation but ways to calm and restore her emotional life. She needs to tend her soul.

Are There Issues You Can't Handle?

When I teach therapists I always ask them to consider the range of their capacity. What kind of issues are too much for them? What kind of people are beyond their reach? Can they help a pedophile? A murderer? Someone who hates women? Someone whose political views are just the opposite of theirs? You not only have to know your limits, but also if you want to be a good therapist, you may have to expand your tolerance. You may have to stretch yourself to be available to more people.

If you are a friend helping someone close to you, you may come up against an issue that presses your buttons. You get upset, at least inwardly, and don't know if you can handle the situation. You have two choices: find a graceful way out or expand your heart. It could be that the issue being presented is particularly difficult for you because of past experiences of your own. In that case, if you can open your mind and heart, you may benefit greatly from offering to help. Usually it is better to step into the fire, where you can find your own catharsis, rather than back away out of fear. But if you do go ahead, you have to be especially careful not to let your own tender emotions get in the way of helping the other person. Jung said that every time you serve as a therapist, you always have to deal with your own issues. In Jung's words (1966), "The doctor must change himself if he is to become capable of changing his patient. We have learned to place in the foreground the personality of the doctor as a curative or harmful factor; and that what is now demanded is his own transformation—the self-education of the educator" (p. 73).

I often tell the story of the chief of psychiatry at the major hospital in the area where I grew up. He visited my father every two weeks. They would sit together in the finished basement of our house and spend two hours together, ostensibly to talk about their stamp collections. From my father's words about the situation I learned that the psychiatrist found a good supervising listener in my father, the plumber. You don't need a degree in psychology to be a good therapist or a therapist's counselor. My father was an excellent accidental therapist, and I'm sure the chief of psychiatry was smart enough to see the potential in him.

But the main point is that the chief of psychiatry found a shrewd way to take care of himself. You need someone to talk to who will protect your privacy and confidentiality, will listen closely, and will make some honest comments. Most of all you need *rapport*, a beautiful French word that means at its base "carrying back and forth." It's a soul word, like *anam cara* and *communitas*, anthropologists Victor and

Edith Turner's word for the inner spark that brings people together. Find someone with whom you have rapport and care for yourself as you care for others.

Deepen Your Pleasures

It can be stressful trying to help a person with matters that confound everybody, like relationships, depression, unfulfilled longings, loneliness, sexual complications, and the need for meaning. Jung said that the therapist should be sorting things out before helping another sort out their life. But that's an ongoing task. No one fully understands himself. So you end up trying to do for someone else what you can't do entirely for yourself. You worry that you aren't competent or ripe enough yet to do the work.

Professional therapists often lack the confidence that they can get to a satisfying place with a client. Many times that concern is justified. They may begin practicing before they are ready. It takes a lot of learning and seasoning to gain confidence. They may also have had a superficial education in the field and need additional study and reading. On the other hand, you have to start sometime, and as long as you are honest with yourself about your training, you can begin. But use a mature psychological supervisor and never stop learning.

The usual forms of relaxation can help. A therapist needs free time, perhaps a sport, travel, exercise, good eating, and sleep. As always, nature offers deep relaxation of mind and heart, so simple walks in a park or in the wilderness can clear out a bottled-up psyche. Marsilio Ficino, the Renaissance magus I often quote, said we should walk near a body of water sparkling in the sun to get some solar spirit in us, and rub laurel leaves. The general point is to choose carefully where you go in nature and get close, close enough to rub the leaves.

I'd also suggest finding a place in nature where you see no signs of civilization. That place would offer what the Greeks called the spirit of Artemis, which is an alternative to intense human interaction. You need some of that pristine spirit washing over you. Notice that you can be thoughtful and imaginative about how to recover from too much human contact, and you may have to do it frequently.

A therapist can also relax through pleasure reading—fiction, detective stories, poetry. Serious studies also can be pleasurable. You could learn about a certain period in art history and soak in the images you find. You could read some classic spiritual texts and find deep comfort in their truths and the ways their insights are formulated. You could learn to understand classical music and deepen your perceptions while enjoying the learning. With these exercises of the imagination you are expanding and deepening the sources of your pleasure.

A therapist might have to relax in ways that have more substance than the mindless escapes people often use. When I suggest good movies and books and the study of art history, I am putting together the pleasure of images and the weight of real study. Of course there is time for ultramindlessness, but in general a therapist who is always "on" needs pleasures that themselves are deep and character building. Pleasure and relaxation don't have to be empty-headed; they could fill your head with rich and satisfying thoughts as they make a day easier.

All sorts of play and games can restore a person and can have deep benefits. Theories about play are so plentiful and rich that you could read about them and be inspired to play games and sports with some depth. I find the books by Timothy Gallwey on the inner games of tennis and golf insightful. Games are full of metaphors that indicate how serious they can be if played with a deeper mind-set than usual. Often they are a special form of contemplation about working through the hazards and reaching the goals of life. It's no accident that the eighteen holes of golf echo the number eighteen, according to the Jewish Kabbalah the number of life.

Meditation, prayer, and ritual can also help restore a therapist spiritually and emotionally. You don't have to belong to any religious or spiritual community to do these things, and they can clear your inner being of many of the knots and preoccupations that have piled up from doing therapy. Just because you no longer go to a church or synagogue does not mean you can't be intensely spiritual (Moore, 2014).

You can make a daily walk into a ritual, which gives it an added, important place in your life. Read Henry David Thoreau (2013) on sauntering. He offers lessons in how to walk with your soul. Among his many strong instructions: "What is it that makes it so hard sometimes to determine whither we will walk? I believe that there is a subtle magnetism in Nature, which, if we unconsciously yield to it, will direct us aright. It is not indifferent to us which way we walk. There is a right way; but we are very liable from heedlessness and stupidity to take the wrong one" (p. 253). The more you make it a meaningful experience, and not just an exercise for your body, the more walking will help you deal with the life issues that come at you every day in therapy.

A good diet helps the body, but the soul also benefits from good dining. Eating can be a meaningful experience not only aimed at physical nourishment but designed for your inner being, as well. Eating traditional food with friends and family members adds to the richness of your life. These aspects also add meaning: eating at a beautiful and striking place; being served well and imaginatively; and learning to cook well. Cooking and presenting food in a special way refines you and makes you more interesting and very human. These activities around food are all good for your soul and can support your work.

A continuing practice of reading good therapists is an immeasurably useful way of gaining confidence in your work. For this book I read Jung, Hillman, Winnicott, Laing, Rogers, and Yalom. I restore my skills by consulting books and videos by Rollo May, Fritz Perls, John Tarrant, Ronald Schenk, Robert Sardello, D. W. Winnicott, Rafael López-Pedraza, Patricia Berry, David L. Miller, John Moriarty, and Nor Hall. I keep certain spiritual books at hand: *Zen Mind, Beginner's Mind, Tao Te Ching, Black Elk Speaks, Upanishads,* Sufi poetry, Jane Hirshfield's *Women in Praise of the Sacred,* and my own translation of the gospels. This is a partial list. I could add many poets and writers of fiction.

Finally, I am always promoting a worldly spiritual life fed

by the world's traditions but not a matter of dogma, moralism, or membership. You may or may not choose to be Catholic or Buddhist or Sufi. The essential thing is to adopt spiritual attitudes and practices that suit you and are intelligent and up-to-date. We will come to a chapter on spirituality soon, but here I emphasize a spiritual vision tailored to your worldview and values that will help you feel centered and comfortable in your role as therapist.

A good therapist takes a person deep into his past or current experiences, and so she has to be at home in the depths. How do you get to that point? You can give serious attention to your night dreams. You can read poets that take you deep, like Jane Hirshfield, Anne Sexton, or Rilke. You can spend time with friends with whom you can discuss your questions and problems. You can watch particularly perceptive films— there are many of them—that will train your imagination so you can go deep with your client. Personally, I calm myself through my friendship with poet Patrice Pinette. Together we explore translations, key words, etymologies, and formats, and I find absolute peace and nourishment in the paintings of my wife, Joan Hanley, and the music of my daughter, Ajeet (Siobhán Moore). I have long, satisfying conversations with my son by marriage, Abraham Bendheim, who is a remarkable architect.

It also helps to have a big vision of your work. You can raise humanity up to a new level of ethical sensitivity. You can help people become more self-contained and purposeful. You can assist people so that they won't be acting out so much in their everyday lives. You can find the roots of rage and anger and ease jealousies. You could find ways to make your understandings more public and therefore so-cially therapeutic. You could see yourself, without egotism, as a therapist for the world.

Oh, Mr. Therapist,
You need a little red suitcase
Full of joys and jokes
and naps and sandwiches
That will keep you smiling
After hearing all those upsetting
Tales of woe and painful wishing.
Keep it close and well stocked
With the things you love.

Chapter 20

A THERAPEUTIC STYLE

When I meet a psychotherapist, the question I want to ask is not "Do you practice therapy?" but "Are you a therapist?" There is a big difference. A therapist's working day is never over. He leaves his building and sees a cleaning person looking sad. "How's life?" he says. "My daughter just learned she's pregnant. She does not know what to do. Can we talk about it?" The therapist goes home, and his children are upset about a bully on the street. He drops everything to help them.

But even in a broader way, you are always a therapist, looking at the many sides of life with an eye for deeper meaning.

Here are some rules of thumb I've picked up since learning that a therapist's workday is never done.

1. You are always "on," always a therapist, always interested in the psyche and observing its behavior. You have a special perspective made up of two elements: depth and

metaphor. In Hillman's language, you always want to "see through," past the literal, the factual, and the practical to deeper needs and issues. You move from layer to layer, always going down into and never coming to an end. Knowing that there is no end to your probing, no answers or conclusions, affects how you look and think. You allow for the mysterious and don't need to end your reflections with answers. As the poet Rainer Maria Rilke (1984) said in an often-quoted passage: "Have patience with everything unresolved in your heart and try to love the questions themselves. . . . Don't search for the answers. . . . Live the questions now. Perhaps then, some day in the future, you will gradually, without even noticing it, live your way into the answer" (p. 34).

2. You have an eye and an ear for metaphor and poetic language. Someone says something, intending to speak at a literal level, and you hear the echoes of other meanings that are more subtle and penetrating. You understand that what really affects the emotions lies far below the obvious.

   You could do this, if you'd like, for every sentence you hear in a day. You ask yourself: *What is he really saying? What does he want that maybe even he does not know he wants? Is he playing me and does not know that he's playing me? What great mythic figure is speaking through the small details of everyday life?*

   You have developed a skill for immediately going deeper and hearing the metaphors. Where others may see facts, you see images, a bigger story and figures that are not personal and human. You feel the presence of the spirits and deities described in spiritual literature. They are not just symbols, nor do they represent parts of the self. They have their own reality in an imaginal realm, not a literal one. You are in tune with that realm. You can live in the dreamworld even in daytime.

3. You don't make therapy too precious. You don't feel inflated, being skillful at recognizing expressions of the soul. You don't present yourself as superhuman. Shunryu Suzuki (1973) made this point in the barest of terms: "The most important thing is to forget all gaining ideas, all dualistic ideas. In other words, just practice zazen in a certain posture. Do not think about anything. Just remain on your cushion without expecting anything. Then eventually you will resume your own true nature. That is to say, your own true nature resumes itself" (p. 49). Apply these principles directly and simply to your caring efforts.

When you meet with people, you let your whole self be seen. You don't hide behind a professional mask but are present as a full person and human being, with your limitations and foibles. You show your ordinary self, while at the same time creating and sustaining the vessel of therapy. You are both ordinary and skilled.

You may not want to go for coffee with your client, but under unusual circumstances you may. You just have to keep the vessel intact. Once, I enjoyed meeting a client at an airport. He would fly in from his home, we'd have our session in a quiet place in the airport, and then he'd fly back home. I never felt that the vessel was broken.

If I am dealing with a particularly shaken person, I keep the boundaries strict and firm, but with most clients I make a point to be present as more than the therapist. I talk a little about my life. If the client asks about how things are going for me, I tell him. I may bring up an experience of mine that seems apropos. I do all this thoughtfully and minimally, just enough to be present as a person. My purpose is to serve the soul of the person I want to help. I hold back my own needs for a different occasion.

4. From the first moment, I'm aware that therapy is a space separate from ordinary conversation. I listen more acutely than usual. I'm tuned in to levels of communication. I listen for the appearance and sound of the soul rather than the intended communication of my client. I hear overtones and reverberations. It's not like listening at ordinary times in life. It's not just focused listening, it's listening for past voices and spirits and angels, to speak metaphorically. I want to know what the soul is seeking and longing for in its complaints and symptoms. I want to be alert to the complexes without getting caught in them.

5. If you are a friend offering an ear, you can easily be yourself and yet create the vessel for a therapeutic conversation. Where you meet may be important. How you talk when therapy begins is significant. Your friend will see that you are creating a space in which she can talk freely and will be heard. You will have to distinguish be-

tween ordinary conversation and therapeutic talking. I'm not alluding to psychological language or anything too formal. You can even be explicit, saying something like, "Okay, let's spend an hour talking about your problem. I'll let you know when the time is up and we can go back to just being friends." Maybe that is too explicit for some situations, but you can adjust it to your needs and style. You could also go to a special private place, and when it feels that the therapy is done for the day, you can get up and go somewhere else.

6. Do you touch your client or friend? Sometimes touching can break the spell of the therapeutic conversation. It may be more satisfying for the therapist than the client. You have to examine your motives and know your habits and needs. But there is no need to fear touching. Your touch can be friendly and warm without crossing any erotic boundaries. If you can't touch that way, don't do it. Don't try it unless you yourself are comfortable and clear. For myself, I rarely touch a client except for a handshake with a man or woman, and even then I usually keep a distance. I'm especially cautious with people who are extremely emotional or easily disturbed.

The highly admired teacher of psychotherapy Irvin Yalom advises not to be afraid of touching but be sensitive and speak about any feelings involved. Sometimes, he says, you might ask a client if they'd like a handshake or a hug. He tells a moving story of how a client had had chemotherapy and had lost most of her hair. He told her he'd like to brush his fingers through the remaining strands. Would it be all right? She said she'd like that. Years later, she told him how important it was to feel good about herself at that moment.

But Yalom (2003) has offered a big caveat: "If I have a concern that my actions may be interpreted as sexual, then I share those concerns openly and make it clear that, though sexual feelings may be experienced in the therapy relationship and should be expressed and discussed, they will never be acted upon. Nothing takes precedence, I emphasize, over the importance of the patient's feeling safe in the therapy office and the therapy hour" (p. 189).

7. You can be an accidental or ephemeral therapist at special moments in ordinary life. A salesperson may ask for some advice in passing, or she may confess to some worry that is getting in the way of serving you. Just a few words indicating that she has been heard and a few more words of clarification may help her. In that brief situation you are being a real therapist, a role that you carry with you. Therapy is portable.

8. Appreciate the sometimes unusual and even bizarre expressions of the psyche. Be slow to judge. Psychologists have an arsenal of labels and diagnoses, and they have to take care not to put people quickly into pathology boxes. A symptom is a precious thing because it tells us that something is wrong and also points to what the psyche needs and wants at that moment. A good therapist learns from a symptom what direction to take. He respects a symptom and does not abuse it by making it sound sick or crazy.

9. I always leave to the client's choice when to meet next, what to talk about, how much time to leave between sessions, and all similar matters. Sometimes I feel an urge to be in control, but then I remember that this is client-centered therapy. It's important to empower clients and also let them deal with the consequence of decisions. I don't need to be in control nearly as much as I might think.

Humor Is a Sign of Soul

A therapist or helping friend can also keep their humor intact. The matter at hand is almost always quite serious, but that does not mean you can't laugh at the human predicament. As people, we are all clowns trying our best to make sense of our lives and do the right thing. But we fail again and again. You can easily laugh at this situation because of its absurdity—everyone taking themselves too seriously and never completely fulfilling their goals. There is a release at realizing you're an ordinary imperfect person who nevertheless has high ideals and wants to do the best you can. That release allows for laughter, and so even at serious moments it's good to allow your sense of humor to show itself. A good humor is one of the main signs of a healthy soul.

I laugh with my clients, never at them, in serious moments, if I grasp the dark humor of the situation, but I pay close attention to their response. I don't want to be laughing alone. Just the right level and tone of humor can breathe some fresh air into a stale problem. I have laughed with people in a psychotic state, people thinking of suicide, people with tears in their eyes due to a painful event. Of course, laughter has to be appropriate in some ways, but it can also broaden the situation and extricate therapist and patient from unnecessary seriousness.

Therapy is not all focused analysis. Once in a while I reach up to my bookshelf and read a quote or a poem that is relevant to what is being discussed. I may do this because I feel a constriction in our conversation. I feel we need a third voice to join us and allow us to look out further from our restricted space. It also models and teaches how good art and literature can be psychologically useful.

Sometimes a client will ask for something that really stretches the container. "Can I stand in the closet while we talk? Behind a curtain?" "May I lie on the floor? Under the couch cushions?" "May I bring my brother to the next session? My girlfriend?" In all these cases, real examples, I said yes. I like to let the client push the boundaries because I want the psyche to show itself. I have limits, but most of the time I take the risk.

As a therapist you have to be flexible, courageous in risk-taking, inventive, open-minded, and adventurous, all the while keeping the vessel sealed. At a deeper level this means not seeing therapy as a formal activity anxiously controlled but as a human relationship, as Rogers would say, in which one person has enough respect for the other that she can help him sort out complex emotional issues.

I also find that working with dreams helps keep the conversations from being too tightly drawn between the two people. The dream is a third thing, another presence, that gives us more space and ease. If you allow an hour's discussion of a dream, it will probably reveal an important insight about the client's life.

My main rule is to love my client's soul. That is not romantic love, because it's not so personal. You see the seeds of what this person could be. You glimpse the tragic events she had to go through, and you feel with her. You sense the promise and the possibilities. Your love of her soul is so intense, the very fulfillment of your vocation, that other kinds of love—romance, sexuality, personal intimacy—do not get in the way. The love of soul is too big and powerful.

> What they don't tell you
> In psychotherapy school
> Is that there are no vacations
> or days off in this work you've
> Decided to do.
> You have a license not just to practice
> But to be.

Chapter 21

PSYCHOTHERAPY AND SPIRITUAL DIRECTION

One day a client of mine, John, told me the saga of how he spent years following one spiritual teacher after another. He started with a guru from India, who turned out to be interested only in money and having docile followers. Then he went to a modern American Sufi community that did not have any focus. Then he converted to Judaism, but he felt that as a half-interested convert he would never be accepted in the community. Finally he became a Catholic, but he felt that he was treated as a child with no thought or judgment of his own. He came to me at the end of his rope.

Was John's problem that he hadn't yet looked in the right place for spiritual leadership, or was there something wrong with the search itself? I felt it was worth exploring the psychological dimensions of his fruitless wanderings instead of taking the spiritual quest on its own terms. I suppose you could go in either direction, but sometimes the psychological seems intuitively more basic.

Let's assume that John was looking for a spiritual home, or just looking for a home. These days the spiritual and religious traditions have roles to play, but they are not good candidates for providing a home. They may add something to a person's spiritual resources, but it has been a long time since you could go to an established church and find a home for your wandering, searching child.

So I turned my attention to John's archetypal child and his personal childhood. Could there be clues there to his adult need for a home? Was he expecting a spiritual community to serve as a parent to his child, and was his frustration not at the inadequacy of each community he tried at being a stellar solution to the problem of meaning but at their failure to give his "child" the security it sought? Spirituality and psychology, spirit and soul, get tightly wrapped up in each other.

Soul and Spirit

A human being is made up of body, soul, and spirit. The word *spirit* here does not refer specifically to a religious kind of spirituality or even to practices like yoga, meditation, and ritual. These forms of spirituality aimed at holiness and perfection are part of the life of spirit, but so are secular endeavors like education, philosophy, scientific exploration, space travel—any activity that seeks to transcend the current status of knowledge and experience. This spirit is one of the three building blocks of a human life.

Soul has entirely different aims and focus. It is the depth of experience that is best expressed in images, dreams, and artworks. It is embedded in ordinary life and prefers intimate experiences like home, family, and close friends. Soul is the source identity of a person, a spring from which a sense of self flows, but the soul itself is bigger than the self and reaches to immeasurable depth. Soul, the ancient writers said, makes us human, while the spirit allows us to transcend our humanity and reach amazing heights and expansions.

Spirit and soul are so close to each other that often it is difficult to tell them apart. One serves and nurtures the other, though they are quite different in nature. It's essential to live in the right part of the world and to have a home that serves as a warm and grounding base for your life—soul. But it's equally useful to travel and get to know other lands and other people—spirit. It's good to have a family spiritual base, but it may also be valuable to experiment with many different spiritual traditions and movements. Spirit and soul are like yin and yang, different and yet intersecting in fruitful ways.

Although psychotherapy is primarily about the soul, it is also directed toward the whole person and therefore can't neglect matters of spirit. Furthermore, ancient writings say that spirit is food for the soul. To care adequately for the soul, you have to give some attention to the spirit. Therefore, all psychotherapists should also be spiritual guides.

Clients often bring up religious issues in telling the stories of their lives. That is one major way in which spirit influences the soul. Old-time religion is not really old-time. Today young people suffer the pressures to believe certain things and to profess values sanctioned by a church and ferried through by the family.

Another shocking way that the spiritual life keeps therapists busy is the paradoxical tendency of some spiritual leaders to exploit those in their care sexually and emotionally. Blatant abuse is common enough, but it is on a spectrum that trails down to control over a person's thoughts and values. We see a tendency among some spiritual leaders to want to dominate others and corral them into a flock of followers. On the other side, there seems to be a strong pull among followers to give over their intelligence and power to a leader with a degree of gullibility difficult to understand.

These two forces—the need to dominate and the tendency to believe anything and follow blindly—are the shadow of spirituality. These trends are so common and so strong that those planning on being a spiritual teacher or a follower should examine themselves carefully lest they fall into these beguiling traps. In other words, for both leaders and followers, especially in critical times in life when you might be launching a career in spiritual direction or deciding to follow a particular teacher, therapy of some kind is in order. At least it is the moment to have a substantial conversation with a friend who knows about such things. But how much better it would be to consult a professional therapist prepared to work with spiritual conversion and vocation.

Spiritual Emotions

Some feelings are so closely connected with the spiritual life that we might call them spiritual emotions: trust, faith, doubt, devotion, obligation, concern about afterlife, innocence, purity, guilt, belonging to a community, betrayal, fear of spiritual authority. A therapist concerned for both spirit and soul could help a client sort out these emotions.

When a person feels insecure and deeply rattled because he can't find a solution to life, a source of comprehensive meaning and a solid direction to take, the resulting state can be profoundly unsettling. The lack of meaning translates into anxiety and the feeling that there is no ground to stand on. In our contemporary world, many people are proud to have grown out of a childish need for organized religion, but they may find themselves without a base on which to stand. They may be unsteady and dizzy from the sudden absence of a platform. They may deal with this anxiety through addictions or multiple marriages or too many career moves, apparently in search of some grounding, but the original loss was too deep for these stopgap solutions. It turns out that the spiritual emotions are more like what we used to call "existential anxiety," which requires a fundamental reorientation in life.

So to look for another religion is not enough. The spiritual emotions are more about being than feeling. Here we can refer to the now common distinction between religion and spirituality. For most people today it is not enough to look for a better religion. The demand is more basic and individual. Now we have to find our own satisfying, livable way of understanding and accept the absolutes that everyone faces: love, health, destiny, and mortality. Each of these concerns is emotional as well as philosophical and theological, and each asks for a deeply important work of imagination—how are you going to make sense of your life, develop solid values, feel secure in your orientation, and finally, deal with the hard fact of your mortality?

The psychological and the spiritual combine in these ultimate concerns and lie, often invisibly, at the base of psychotherapy. What seems to be a psychological issue is often a spiritual one, and vice versa. Speaking as a seasoned psychotherapist, I don't see how fellow therapists can deal adequately with a client, no matter how superficial the presenting problem appears, without having faced these ultimate matters themselves. The religions offer hints to solutions, but in the end, spiritually, people have to arrive at answers for themselves. Or, with Rilke in mind, we might say that the search is for good questions and deep ways of pondering them.

I see no other conclusion: a psychotherapist is by definition also a spiritual director.

To me, afterlife is a serious issue. People have many different thoughts about it, but everyone, I'm sure, has to come up with a livable answer and solution. I remember a tense moment in my friendship with James Hillman. We were standing in a hallway in his house in Connecticut, letting our minds roam. It was about one year before his death, as I recall. Out of the blue he said to me, "About an afterlife, I'm a materialist. There is nothing to expect."

I was surprised at this declaration, which sounded like a

final conclusion. Here was a man who all his life advocated taking into account the invisible powers directing life and culture, powers he often described using the images of the Greek gods and goddesses. His summary of religion at the end of his major work *Re-Visioning Psychology* (1975b) is a model of cautious, open-minded faith. Even Jung, Hillman's spiritual father in many respects, when asked if he believed in God, famously said, "Belief is difficult. I don't believe. I know."

I understood that Hillman always avoided a sentimental solution to anything. He did not want to be at all gullible or wishful in his thinking. He wrote a lot about the spiritual, but his writing is usually critical. It bothered me that he referred to "Christianism" rather than Christianity, making it a despised ideology rather than a neutral theological movement. I have huge complaints about Christianity, but I treasure its rich thought, effective rituals, transformative art, and inspiring means of meditation, devotion, and contemplation. So Hillman and I parted in our approach to the spiritual. I don't know if he could have been effective as a psychotherapist if he had had to deal with a client's spiritual conundrums.

On the other hand, in spite of his biases he was a dedicated and astute theological thinker. He would have been, I expect, a good existentialist adviser about spiritual matters but not favorable toward the traditions. I have a different approach. I admire and respect the many traditions and have tried to adopt the teachings of many different traditions that make sense to me.

On occasion Hillman would refer to me disdainfully as a "monk," sometimes because he thought I was not worldly enough or concerned enough about money, sometimes because I was more favorably disposed toward the spiritual traditions. So this is where we diverged, and I mention it only to bring focus to the ways spirit and soul intersect in the work of therapy.

Clients in therapy are often searching for meaning, or they may be suffering from emotional wounds from their childhood experience of religion. We are still in an era when hard religious upbringing remains in the memories of adults. These are tenacious and often burrow deep into the psyche.

Religious and spiritual ideas can also drag a person down when these ideas have not matured and become more sophisticated as the person ages. Most of us evolve in our technological skills and our understanding of what is going on in society, but religion often remains stuck in a childhood phase. Many people believe exactly what they were taught as children.

But religious attitudes today can be mature and precisely appropriate. James Hillman offered an example of this new mature religiousness in his positive directions for prayer in a time of too much or not enough belief:

Psychotherapy stops short. It invites confession but omits prayer. The religious impulse is provoked and then unsatisfied. A secondary religious aura then pervades many aspects of psychotherapy. Analysis itself is regarded religiously; "experience" is endowed with religious values, becoming sacred, unavailable to examination: the dogma of experience. The emotions of the heart are taken for religious revelations. . . .

Prayer offers a therapy of confession. By praying we move out. As Coleridge insisted, the intensity of Western subjectivism requires a personal divinity to whom we address our hearts. We are saved by these divinities, psychologically, for we are saved from the personalism of feeling by bringing those feelings to persons who are not we, who are beyond our notion of experience. They who are they. They who give experience and are its ground, so that the himma in the heart [images taken as real, though not physical] recognizes them, and not ourselves, as the true Persons. We talk to them, they to us and this "dialogical situation" which constitutes prayer (in distinction to idolatry, worship, ecstasy) as a psychological act is "the supreme act of the creative imagination" [1981, pp. 23–24].

The Therapist as Spiritual Director

Therapists would be better prepared if they were educated in matters of spirit. They don't have to be full-fledged spiritual masters and teachers or theologians, but they should know enough about spirituality to help their clients navigate it. They don't need a degree in religious studies, but they need to be aware of the importance of spiritual issues and how they affect psychological ones.

Say the client's ties with a church begin to pull apart. The teachings don't make sense any longer, or the client feels empty going to a church where the language and customs no longer inspire her. She may feel hypocritical when inwardly she can no longer believe in it. The result may be a feeling of loss and sadness and the wish for a new kind of support. She now knows what it's like not to have a source of meaning, and she needs some help at this turning point.

Who does she go to for support then? She can't go to the old church leaders, a priest, rabbi, or minister. She can't just find an alternative community of faith. Yet her feelings are deep and difficult. Meaning, values, and purpose have strong emotions attached to them. The client's painful feelings are not about relationships or interpersonal conflicts. They aren't about work or depression or anxiety in the usual sense. They are related to a loss of a belief structure. She is suddenly on her own, and that is not the way she has lived. She needs a new strategy and something new to believe in.

It would be helpful to find a therapist who knows about spiritual doubt and seeking, and who appreciates the emotional turmoil that loss of faith can stir up. It would be even better if that therapist had some acquaintance with several religious or spiritual teachings. Some people feel as if they are drifting and depressed and don't realize immediately what is wrong. They may not connect spiritual floating with emotional pain, and it is not easy for them to find a therapist who is open and skilled to work with deep spiritual emotions.

The Basics of Spiritual Guidance

The first requirements for a spiritually alert therapist are open-mindedness and an appreciation for spiritual teachings and practices. Some therapists show little interest in spiritual matters and aren't terribly sophisticated about them. They assume that their job is to convert the client to their own values and beliefs, which tend toward either fundamentalism or agnosticism. They may act as witness to their belief or unbelief. But, assuming that the task in therapy is to help individuals clarify their emotions and thoughts, this approach is not therapeutic.

Imposing your values and beliefs is a cultural habit that we need to reassess. At its best, the desire to convert others may stem from the benefits you have received from your path. But when the need to convert is strong, you may spot some insecurity at its base. Strong, vocal belief may be a cover for doubt and uncertainty. Life is complicated, and a simple set of morals and spiritual ideas may not be adequate. The need to convert may stem from a need to find validation and support to overcome your anxiety.

Even an open-minded therapist may quietly try to convince his client of his own answers. His prejudice may be so hidden and slight that it goes unnoticed and plays out subliminally. Avoiding obvious proselytizing, this therapist may nevertheless try to persuade his client to be open-minded.

On the positive side, a therapist can help a client sort out his spiritual history, its influences, and even some of the emotional issues wrapped up in belief. The client may become more spiritually mature through this sorting process and discover ways of being spiritual that are satisfying to the adult and not just leftovers from childhood. The therapist does not come up with a solution but rather gathers together the many elements that have gone into the client's position, and this collection clarifies things for the client.

Appreciate Religion

The pattern I have just described is often quite the opposite. Some therapists in favor of cultural and spiritual diversity find it difficult to appreciate a client who is dedicated to an established religion. But if you are going to be open-minded, should you not respect a person's devotion to their family tradition or to a newfound religious home? We all are at some point on our journey, and for many reasons, now may be the time to join an established, perhaps traditional spiritual community. Being free and independent is not always an evolutionary move in the spiritual journey but an option, as is choosing to join a church.

You can understand a person today turning to traditional religion not so much as clinging to the truth as exploring the spiritual universe. Personally, I lived the traditional route intensely from day one. Then I was a monk for twelve years. I know that life and loved it. Now I move in a different direction, and yet my monastic life is still part of me and affects my lifestyle and values. I am Catholic at heart, even though today the political stances the Church often takes discourage me from participating much. The exaggerated authoritarianism is completely unnecessary and intimately connected to a fear of women and the worldly life. I would like to see a Catholic Church made up of small communities without clergy and certainly without the vast authoritarian pyramid structure.

But I can appreciate someone becoming a Catholic today. I can see it as a move forward in their spirituality. They may be able to focus on the rich spirituality and not be bothered by all the rest. If I am counseling them, I want to be open to their choice. They sometimes come to me precisely because of my Catholic background and my knowledge of that tradition. People may select you for a similar reason. They may want someone who understands agnosticism or Judaism or just being a seeker.

Learn About the World's Spiritualities

The next step is an easy one: become familiar with the basic insights of many spiritual traditions. In graduate school I heard it said, "If you know one religion, you know none." It is a momentous step to stand outside your familiar spiritual position and open yourself to the views of another. As a therapist, you can easily find a good translation of the gospels, the *Tao Te Ching*, the Old Testament, Sufi poems, Native American prayers and songs, Buddhist sutras such as the life-transforming Heart Sutra, and Jewish prayers. You can go a long way by just reading and rereading these basic texts and perhaps reading some good commentaries. You can listen to a gifted speaker from one of many traditions. Then you are ready to help people with their spiritual emotions. You have to educate yourself in spiritual matters, but you don't need a degree.

You can go further than just being open to the spiritual teachings of the world. You can take them to heart, the essence or parts of them, anyway, and discover for yourself how they give your psyche the vision and principles you need. You can love the teachings and know them well. Then you would be prepared to help your clients with their spiritual development, and that is a great plus for any therapist.

Don't Be Anti-Intellectual

When I was just becoming a therapist, I had studied the gospels closely, had read Paul Tillich and Pierre Teilhard de Chardin and Thomas Merton, had read the collected works of Jung, had studied James Hillman intensely. I had gone through hands-on training in Carl Rogers's client-centered therapy, had participated in many Gestalt therapy sessions, and had had the opportunity to lead groups in therapy under supervision. Yet I felt it was the reading and intense study that really prepared me. I confess, I live much of my life through books, even though my Gestalt teachers were wary of the intellectual life. Fritz Perls himself, the creator of Gestalt therapy, was quite an intellectual, and Carl Rogers, too, for all his emphasis on relationship had a strong background in ideas, having attended Union Theological Seminary.

The best foundation for a good therapist is to be schooled in excellent ideas. Of course, you don't try to deal with highly emotional problems in a purely intellectual way, but you can rely on a solid foundation in good ideas about human experience and how to support it effectively. To be prepared for this difficult work, you have to study and have a deep grounding in psychological thought. It would not hurt to become a thoughtful philosopher, as well. Among the best therapists I know are practical philosophers, not just philosophical therapists.

Avoid Contention

Spiritual people can be contentious and touchy about language and beliefs. They argue easily or dismiss others without grounds, often for superficial reasons. This is all part of the psychopathology of spiritual experience, a widespread problem that hasn't been studied enough in depth.

As a therapist or counselor, you might examine yourself about this common tendency to be argumentative and dismissive in the face of beliefs and ideas that are not part of your own system. When you feel defensiveness rise up in you as you listen to your client or friend, relax and allow the diversity. If you feel angry when you hear ideas that are unfamiliar, ease up. You have nothing to fear. Let the other person have their own spiritual journey and discoveries. Does anyone have the final, absolute answers?

Various religions and spiritual approaches use strikingly different words, but on closer inspection you find that their ideas are a lot like your own. Personally I don't use the word *God*. I think it is overused and can be misleading. Many people seem to have God pinned down. But I know that the word can be used with great openness, and so I don't get upset when I hear it. Still, I do have a sliver of atheism in me that keeps me honest.

On the other hand, I can also be evangelical and fundamentalist in my own way. For the most part I feel quite open and have learned much from many traditions. Yet I am prickly about some words and ideas. I have to be careful when I'm counseling someone with different ideas and language, because I can feel too certain. I can be rigid in my own way and recognize this as the shadow of my open-mindedness about spiritual diversity.

Be Fed Spiritually by Unfamiliar Traditions

You can also keep in mind how the psychological and the spiritual blend into each other. People may latch on to a spiritual teaching for psychological reasons, and vice versa, they may help their emotional life by clarifying their spiritual vision. Both of these directions are crucial in doing therapy. You can assist as your clients sort out the pieces that come together in creating a comforting and inspiring spiritual path.

It could also be useful if you had considered and practiced many ways of being spiritual outside formal communities and traditions. In this the transcendentalists of New England offer much practical advice and modeling. Emerson, Thoreau, and Emily Dickinson were all dedicated to an intense non-denominational spiritual practice, each somewhat different in approach but all of them also writing about their ideas and practices. Every therapist would benefit from having copies of their books within sight during a therapy hour.

People often turn to their priest, minister, rabbi, or other spiritual leader for help with life's conundrums and trage-dies. Many have training in counseling and feel and indeed are capable of working therapeutically when they need to. Others feel insecure because they haven't had formal train-ing. Some have training, but it is not adequate, because clergy often have to deal with difficult cases.

If I were teaching fledgling priests and ministers, I would present their vocation as one of offering therapeutic attention in all that they do: leading prayer and ritual, offering comfort to the sick and those who have lost loved ones, at marriage and life's turning points, in ritual. As I said, you find the word *therapy* frequently used in the gospels, and in Islam, Buddhism, and Judaism you also find strong teachings and images for care.

When I want to be reminded of what therapy is essentially, I usually reread the last few pages of Plato's dialogue *Euthyphro*. There Socrates and a student discuss two related words: *therapeia* and *hosion*. *Therapeia*, of course, is "therapy," and *hosion* is sometimes translated as "holiness." To me, the best definition of holiness or piety that we get in this dialogue is "doing what is pleasing to the gods." Socrates uses the intriguing phrase *therapeia theon*, "therapy of the gods."

With these few thoughts in the background, I would conclude that therapy means caring for the relationship people have with the law of their own nature and the laws of life. To be in tune with their hearts and living as close as possible to the example of the natural world. To be who you are essentially, not contradicting what it means to be either a human being or you.

The role of the clergy is not primarily to teach a particular set of ideas or rules but to help people stay in line with their own natures. To do what is pleasing to God or the gods and goddesses.

The clergy also represent and carry the divine, the infinite, and the mysteries. They embody holiness and therefore can teach by example how to live both spiritually and soulfully.

Their role, then, is highly compatible with the work of the therapist, and we could go on to say that ordinary people not only can practice therapy in an extended sense but also can be spiritual guides: teachers for their students, parents for their children, and ordinary people for their friends and neighbors.

Needless to say, I'm not talking about proselytizing, converting people to your beliefs, or moralizing according to your own values. You can embody and demonstrate your own transcendent vision and help others with this important part of life through deep conversation. Indeed it is a touching thing, because today many spiritual people feel a need to convert others to their point of view. It seems difficult to help people with their spiritual lives freely and openly. But if the clergy can achieve this important viewpoint, they have much to offer therapeutically to people who naturally come to them for guidance.

The meditating monk
Sits on the point of a steeple
Like Socrates looking for higher thoughts,
Loving the vertigo of perching
In midair admiring the view,
Nothing all around.

Chapter 22

A THERAPIST'S SHADOW

We therapists are generally decent people. We are in this work to help, and we enjoy spending many hours guiding people through tough times. However, it's easy for us to get a high opinion of ourselves and to believe that we are nothing but good. All this sets us up for surprising and difficult confrontations with our shadow sides.

Shadow is a term Jung used to describe that complex figure within us who embodies all the bad stuff that we keep out. But the shadow is not always objectively bad. For some people anger and sexuality are their shadows, while for others these are just part of life, even positive. The Jungian shadow lies just below the surface and can be made part of life without long analysis and challenging work. According to Jung, dealing with shadow might be the first step you take toward retrieving your soul.

Some do talk about "integrating" the shadow and make it sound too easy. But you don't exactly integrate the shadow.

Over years you come to know your dark side, never reaching a full reconciliation, of course. Shadow is vast. At one level it acts like a complex made up of much repressed material, but it also has an archetypal dimension. Human beings are never perfect, and they are never wholly good and innocent. There is personal shadow, and there is human shadow.

Some shadow material arises because of the circumstances of our family and upbringing. Intense religious instruction that is moralistic may convince a person to try to be good at all costs and to adopt a manner that is clean and spotless. Other people may have little of that influence and take the shadow side as being quite ordinary. Therefore, some of us have to work harder than others with the shadow.

People trying to keep the shadow away sometimes have disturbing dreams of overflowing toilets or other bathroom experiences. In the dream they may do everything possible to keep from being soiled, an image that is not difficult to appreciate in psychological terms. The dreamer may be tempted to think that the dream wants her to be cleaner, whereas it is likely showing her how she goes to extremes to avoid being tarnished and soiled. The dream is an invitation to stop avoiding the messy aspects of living a human life.

Therapists Have a Shadow

Therapists have specific shadow qualities that go with the profession. They like to appear somewhat above the human condition and may give the impression that they have solved all their problems. They may hide their shadow behind their credentials and reputation. It is not unusual for a client to assume that his therapist has dealt with all human struggles effectively and cleanly. In my practice, when I notice these attitudes coming into the foreground, I don't actively counter them. I remain neutral and presume that neutrality will deprive them of oxygen.

Good therapists are well-acquainted with their shadow material without being discouraged by it. They can live with it and even, under somewhat limited conditions, reveal it to their clients. Allowing your clients to see some of your shadow can help them deal with theirs. If you make an effort to be clear and shadow-free, they won't be encouraged to accept their dark tendencies. As we have seen many times, you have to do several things at once: show that you have reached a good level of self-understanding and calm, and also show some of your failings and less noble inclinations.

The informal therapist may also have shadow material to deal with. He may think too highly of himself and therefore make himself available to others out of his hubris. Or he may confuse therapy with advice and preach at people from his own exalted values. He may need intimacy in his own life and find it with his clients. His clients' problems may make him feel superior, a need of his own fulfilled by those who seek his counsel. The list of shadow qualities is long, and a lay therapist has to reflect on his intentions at least as much as the professional.

A great deal of energy and attention can go into control of the shadow, and the shadow's suppression amounts to hiding a major part of one's being. A therapist who can't let her shadow be present can't be fully there for her client. Yet a therapist is often caught between wanting to be a kind and helpful companion on one side and a full human being on the other.

The Content of a Therapist's Shadow

A good, often discussed example of a therapist's shadow is money. Some therapists confess that as they are listening to a client's tales of woe, they are thinking about how much money they are making during the hour and then for the year. As the client's tales of disaster pour forth, the therapist might be watching the clock to be finally free of captivity, using a mental calculator working out his bank account. The therapist may offer a sliding scale of fees, but the shadow of that gift is a hunger for more money. Some therapists make a show of their generosity and then complain at the slightest hitch in getting paid. Money is the golden road to the shadow.

You need a way to understand shadow and strategies for dealing with it effectively. The first step is obvious: you have to acknowledge the feelings and thoughts you have. It's tempting to avoid them because they don't make you feel good about yourself. A psychological supervisor for the professional is a valuable resource for matters of shadow. No matter how much you know about the theory of shadow, it's difficult to face the actual material by yourself and own it. Another person can be the midwife, helping your shadow emerge into awareness.

The key to working with shadow is to understand that

it is not literal corruption. The therapist who counts her fees and hours should not change entirely and forget about money. Just the opposite, this preoccupation, a sign that her thoughts are symptomatic, shows that she does not think about money enough or in the right ways. You never try to get rid of shadow, you deepen it. When money is the problem, it is also the solution. I'd rather go to a therapist who can handle money up front and effectively, even if she has some shadow around it, than one for whom money is mostly symptomatic.

Shadow behaviors are most destructive when they remain internal, when the therapist is not aware of them or does not confront them. It can be a great relief to tell your shadow tendencies to someone who will not judge you but will help you clarify what is going on. It can be a miraculous, liberating moment when a therapist tells her supervisor about her shadow qualities for the first time, finally unburdened and ready to move ahead. If you don't deal with the shadow, it could interfere with the therapy and even with a professional career.

Another shadow aspect—Guggenbühl-Craig (1976) mentions it in *Power in the Helping Professions*—is the salvation fantasy, sometimes known as "the savior complex." A therapist may confuse clarifying with saving. It is an enlargement or swelling of the therapist's job and purpose. He helps clarify and works alongside his client, but he does not save the person. You might also call this a Jesus complex, the sense that you are in possession of the key to life and can save anyone who believes in you.

In this case the savior hero is the shadow figure, and he is difficult to recognize. We live in a heroic society where every issue is a problem to be solved or an enemy to be overcome. In that spirit, the therapist may see herself as the Neurosis Czar who wages a war on emotional discomfort and life struggles. It's fine to be fired up with belief in your work and your education, but the complex is an added element that makes the whole project neurotic.

Instead, the therapist could say to his client: "I am here to serve the needs of your soul, to be with you as you try to make sense of your life. I know some things, but I am also in need of salvation, if anyone is. I am the White Knight whose armor is rusted and dented. I am the nonhero, the antihero. Actually, there is not a heroic bone in my body. Like you, I am a simple human being trying to get along. It would be my honor to join you in your serious quest for happiness."

Working with Shadow

In dealing with shadow, let's use our rule of thumb: go with the symptom. Therapists preoccupied with the money they are making at the work could, for example, put more attention on the business of doing therapy professionally. It's fine to be concerned about money and business. We all worry about money and would like to make more of it. But when you suppress these thoughts they become less reasonable and may rise up at awkward moments. The symptom does not tell you to get rid of your concern about money but to tend to it thoughtfully, admit your need for money, and become skilled at dealing with it.

Enter into the symptom. Learn what it is asking from you. The first solution to this shadow problem is to face it, sort it out, and find a way to be an honest and caring therapist and at the same time work at being successful at your business.

In general, shadow requires personal strength and the capacity to confront yourself. It may help to expect some shadow element in every positive experience. The more glowing the value, the more likely its shadow will be quite dark. You could be a shadow specialist, someone who understands how everything good has its dark side, and you know the subtleties of dealing with it.

If you are having sexual fantasies that worry you, again go with the symptom. Be a more sexual and sensual person, inside and outside your practice of therapy. Speak comfortably about sex when it comes up. Show that you are someone interested in it in general. Be more interested. Read about it. Make dealing with sexuality one of your strengths as a therapist. Don't present an image of virtue and bodylessness. Maybe your problem is not your sexuality but your half-in, half-out attitude toward it.

Integrating the shadow is not an abstract or simple process. It means going deep into the theme of the shadow and finding effective ways to live it.

Shadow Is a Good Thing Begging for Fuller Expression

Another big shadow issue for therapists is ignorance. Therapists may be afraid to say, in answer to a question, "I don't know." Some become self-important and inflated with the knowledge they have. Others go too far in obtaining various credentials that stand in for actual knowledge, and blazon their degrees.

A good therapist does not operate from the seat of his pants. He's interested in deep thoughts about the material he deals with in therapy. He wants to know more. It might help if he were to distinguish factual knowledge from insight, as we discussed earlier. I also pointed out that, for me personally, good ideas give me confidence. I'm not so interested in techniques or slogans or an evidence-based approach. I think a therapist best prepares for the work by studying human nature deeply and letting the practical lessons emerge in therapy with a unique client. Sometimes it's better to read philosophy or novels than books on psychology. When I was first starting out, colleagues jokingly referred to me as the "practical philosopher." I took that as a compliment.

Confidence can be an elusive quality for therapists. They feel they don't know enough. In response, they may look for simple techniques easy to apply, or simple diagnoses, simple solutions. But life is complex, so a simple method, though satisfying and giving the illusion of knowledge and skill, may be a defense. It might be better to really study and train for dealing head-on with complexity by using sophisticated methods.

The fact is, you are indeed ignorant and will never know fully how people work. We are all ignorant. You will never be a completely confident therapist, but you can have enough trust in yourself to do the work comfortably. If ignorance is your shadow, you have to go into it and be guided by it. Anxious ignorance eases when you admit that you will never know enough.

But at the same time you can appreciate and display your knowledge and experience. You can be confident in your skills. The two, ignorance and knowledge, are only effective when they work together. A client knows that you are intelligent and skillful but have your limits and can admit to them—a good combination.

Necessary Loss of Innocence

You may have to leave your blank, uncomplicated, and naïve innocence behind. Therapists, again intending good and in a "helping" profession, may have too much self-esteem. Their high opinion of themselves and their profession can create a dark shadow where their mistakes, lack of education, and personal inadequacies lie hidden.

A thoughtful person once gave me some feedback that I took to heart. She told me I should not be so innocent when I present ideas that challenge accepted assumptions about religion and emotional health. I'm questioning the establishment and provoking my readers to reconsider their allegiances. I should do it all with less innocence, she said. For years now, when giving a lecture, that woman's voice comes back to me, and I make an effort to acknowledge the shadow in my role of gadfly.

Therapy is not a fully innocent occupation. You challenge, advocate for toughness and independence, tell clients to confront their spouses and bosses. If you are out of touch with the shadow in your own job and persona, the contradiction may weaken your work.

It is not a matter of innocence versus shadow. As in all such patterns we've discussed, the best solution is a blend of the two split elements. You need to be darkly innocent or suitably in touch with shadow. Innocence does not have to disappear, but it does need maturing. The ultimate goal is a paradox, and as you act on your mature innocence, you feel the paradox in your body. You know you are doing two things at once. You present yourself as a complicated adult. You can be trusted because you are not obviously and completely trustworthy.

The False Shadow

Finally, some people avoid the shadow by embodying its darkness. They may "integrate" their shadow by being rough-spoken, scraggly-haired, unkempt, sexually leering males. Women have their counterparts. Therapists may know a little about shadow and think that by being rough and dark they exhibit shadow in a way that resolves the issue.

In classical psychoanalysis, identification is a form of defense. In this case a person may take on shadow characteristics, looking and behaving tough, but all the while he is far from his shadow in any real sense. Like most defenses, it is clever and misleading. The shadow qualities you exhibit defensively are not real. They are playacting as a defense. The real shadow would come from deep inside you and may not look so ugly. The visibly rough quality of the false shadow betrays its insincerity. A real shadow quality is integral to who you are and appears in serious ways, not as a facade.

The false shadow is also apotropaic. That means warding

off, keeping away. You put up a scarecrow to keep the birds away from the corn. You dress up like the shadow to keep the real shadow at bay. Those rough-looking therapists are probably softies at heart. They don't know how to be really tough and strong in dealing with the major issues that confront people. A tough exterior usually covers over a mushy interior.

An alternative solution is to allow your shadow to accompany you. You can't really integrate it, but you can befriend the shadow, drawing on her characteristics and powers. This shadow can strengthen you and complete you, but she will always be other, never simply an interesting and useful side of your self. One day the shadow will be the companion at your side, completing your view of the world and allowing you to deal with real people, who need your shadow as well as your virtue.

Today I met my twin,
The one who follows me around
When the sun is bright.
I've never liked him
But he seems to love me
And his good side is growing on me.

Chapter 23

THE POWER OF THE THERAPEUTIC

If you were to read the writings of good therapists like Rogers and Yalom, you might be surprised at how slow they are to advise and analyze their clients. An amateur helping a friend might be even more cautious about telling him what to do or what is going on with him. The other thing you might notice with these expert therapists is that they frequently ask their patient if they want to explore various themes and how they feel about what has happened in therapy. These therapists don't force themselves on their patients but rather invite collaboration in everything. "Would you like to talk about this?" they will say. "How would it feel if I suggested some reading?"

Therapy Is an Art

These therapists are also clear about their own feelings and behavior. They might say quite plainly, "I hesitated to bring up this issue in case you would be upset." Or, "I feel that we are becoming friends, but I want to keep some distance so we can do our work cleanly." Personally, I try to make therapy an art, and that means being thoughtful about every action and word without becoming too self-conscious. I always remember that therapy begins with the hello and ends with good-bye. Everything that happens in between is grist for the mill, part of the material we have to deal with.

A therapeutic conversation is not ordinary, unconscious talk. It is artful exchange, done for a specific purpose and for the benefit of the one being helped and not the helper. You speak thoughtfully, honestly, and genuinely. You are witnessing what you say and do so even as you speak. You have a therapist personality at work watching what is going on so you can do the work with skill. The talking is almost artificial, its aim not the same as ordinary conversation. You have to keep in mind that you have summoned the mythic therapist to do the work. You are not talking off the top of your head.

The psychotherapist is one who speaks to and for the soul. That is the meaning of the word *psychotherapy*. You take care with your words and your behavior so that you build the vessel of therapy as an environment for soul work. You don't have to be a professional, but you do have to be unusually watchful and aware. You not only love the person you're working with, you also love the work. It is the power of that love that generates healing.

If we can get beyond the idea that therapy is counseling for specific life problems and see it as constant care for the soul of people, organizations, places, and things, then we might imagine living therapeutically as a general principle. We are always in a position to offer deep care for whatever is under consideration.

As I said before, I try to be therapeutic when I write my books. That does not mean I want to solve problems or fix what is broken or advise people in managing their daily lives and relationships. I have a larger sense of the therapeutic. I am a servant of the soul. That is my calling and it could be yours. You could live a therapeutically oriented life, bring deep care wherever you go. You could be vastly interested in the psyche and the ways of the soul. Then, no matter what your job or career, your lifework would be a form of therapy. Therapy does not have to be bottled in a particular label or language or profession. You can be therapeutic when you write a letter or email, or when you speak to a business associate or a customer, or when you say good night to your children. Therapy is appropriate every moment of every day. You are not fixing the world, but you are giving it the care it needs to thrive.

Bringing Power to People

Many therapists, when asked why they entered the profession, say, "I wanted to be in a job where I could help people." I have heard this statement many times over the years, and I am always impressed with its simplicity and sincerity. Practicing therapy can give both the professional and the amateur the sense that their life is worthwhile for having helped people deal with stresses and conflicts or bringing them deeper into themselves.

One of my life principles is this: if I am feeling a loss of meaning or value, all I have to do is offer care to someone else in need. If a therapist is more concerned about her own knowledge or skills or position, she won't do the best job possible and therefore will not gain its rewards.

Therapy can also empower people receiving your care to be more effective in life and therefore happier. Power of soul is not about control over other people but about living from a deep place and finding there the ability to transform the world. This kind of power is not force or control but effectiveness, strength, and confidence, powers that are always with you.

Real power is not the same as ego strength. It comes more from allowing the forces of life to flow through you and make your work effective. People are confused about this fundamental law of life and are often dismayed when control over people does not give them the satisfaction they crave. To be truly powerful you have to be open to influence and able to allow the force of life to do your job. It is more about getting out of the way and finding skills to accommodate the mysterious forces in life that are present. Good therapists do not manipulate their clients' lives to serve the values of the therapist; instead, they show their clients how to tap into the life forces that can make them effective and strong.

Most conflicts in life have some masochism in them. That means that problems arise when people lose touch with the powers around them that can make them creative and productive and strong in relationships. To be healed is to reconnect with the positive powers and feel them flowing through you and having their push behind you in everything you do. This kind of power resolves problems and restores happiness.

You can ask yourself which abilities allow you to live a meaningful life. To persuade, create, nurse, manage, rule, entertain, educate? One of them is the power to be therapeutic. If you can offer care in a way that restores meaning and confidence in people, you have a power of great value to society and to other people. You are making an important contribution and you should feel good about your life and your place in society. You don't need any further motivation to become part of the therapeutic professions or to offer your talents to neighbors and relatives in an informal way.

The Greeks said Love is an adolescent boy
Carrying a quiver of arrows
that he does not hesitate to shoot.
That's no metaphor.
I've seen him and have been shot.
He hides in corners and behind bushes
Striking when I wish he wouldn't.

Chapter 24

THE THERAPIST IN EVERYONE

A professional therapist has to cultivate a position in the community as a skilled resource for people in psychological distress. But we all are called upon rather frequently to be there for family members, spouses, friends, and coworkers. At the death of a loved one, just before a marriage, at the loss of a job, when depression hits—there are many times when the sheer company of a caring friend gets you through a dark night of the soul.

But people sometimes feel inadequate when they want to help. They don't know what to say, how to be of use, or when to intercede. It would be useful to have some education in how the psyche works and how to deal with strong emotions. Natural care is valuable, but enlightened care is even better.

Understand that there is a therapist in you. You can go some distance, not like a professional, but with your own talents and/or ordinary ways toward helping someone deal with tragedy, conflict, and pain.

In fact, your lack of a professional license or position could help you be with a friend in a way less challenging than the professional route. The trust is probably there already. A relationship exists. The whole experience can be just part of life without the anxieties associated with formal therapy. Even your inexperience can be an advantage.

Therapists in Disguise

Recently I was speaking with a man who was considering whether to take a course with me in depth psychology. I had just been saying how I feel that I am a therapist in most things that I do. Even as a writer, I express myself as a therapist. I'm not just interested in ideas for their own sake. I want rich sources to dig into for showing how the psyche works and how to deal with its complaints and symptoms. So the man said, "I probably should not take the course. I'm a lawyer."

I was shocked. "You're a lawyer," I said. "You probably counsel people more than I do. You need the course, because you need some psychological sophistication in dealing with the intense situations you run into." In my view, the lawyer was certainly at least 50 percent therapist.

I understand that we have a tendency to divide up professions anxiously into discrete, well-differentiated compartments. We want to keep everyone separate according to their specialties. But there is no getting around the fact that lawyers need a well-functioning therapist in them. You can imagine this particular definition of therapist I am using as a set of skills, a persona that you can identify with, or an identity that fits you well among other identities.

Other partial therapists might include teachers, managers, cab and limo drivers, doctors, hospice workers, bartenders, and parents. As I said before, I don't mean to confuse the roles but to point out that many professions involve counseling people, whether customers, associates, or underlings. All sorts of businesses would do well to have some psychological instruction as part of their training. I wish my doctor would go to a course in depth psychotherapy.

The idea is not to have a new degree in psychology but to know the basics of therapy. Some lessons in listening, complexes, transference, and symptoms would help. Some spiritual ideas on meaning, purpose, morality, and values could raise informal counseling to a remarkable level. Everyone could benefit from lessons in listening, the alchemy of sorting things through, and the purpose of symptoms. Constructive ideas on the shadow side of the psyche would go a long way toward turning advice-giving into genuine therapy.

The Informal Vessel

An ordinary person when asked to help a relative at a time of emotional upset could think first about the vessel. *Where and when should we talk? How should I present myself? Could I assure my cousin of my confidentiality?*

Your cousin phones and says, "I'm finalizing my divorce. I'm anxious and have bellyaches. I can't sleep. I just need someone to talk to."

You are not a therapist, but you would like to help your cousin. The first issue to think about is who you are and what you can do. You can remind him that you are not a professional therapist, but you are willing to listen and try to offer some insight and support. You start with making it clear who you are and what your intentions are.

Your cousin suggests meeting at his favorite diner. Now you have to think about the vessel. Is his favorite diner the best place? He may know people there and not feel private enough. The place may be too loud and busy. You think about it and recommend that you meet at a park and start with a walk. Walking can promote conversation and is usually quite private. You can imagine a vessel around the two of you as you walk where there is privacy and you talk quietly.

Next your cousin says, "I always thought about you as a father to me." This is in the first few sentences of your role as an informal therapist, and already you have a hint of the archetypal father entering the picture. You hear his statement as saying more than he intends. You have to be ready to bear the role of father and both the good and the bad that role entails.

As you get into a deep conversation, you will have many other challenges. Adapt the many suggestions and warnings in this book to your informal therapeutic conversations. You can become more skillful and sophisticated about the psyche. We know a little about what is going on when our computer does not work right or our car is running loud, but we have no idea about the psyche. We may not even hear the psyche when it is too loud. No one taught us. It was not on the curriculum. So you have to educate yourself.

The Intruders

Let's review some of the more difficult challenges that may come up in informal therapeutic conversations.

Sometimes a long-standing pattern or script creeps into a discussion, and the helping friend may not realize that the person in front of him is not really the one speaking to him. Instead, some strong emotion or maybe even a whole complex of emotions has intruded upon the conversation. I prefer to speak of an intrusion rather than an invasion, because often you don't notice the arrival of something new and quite autonomous.

The cousin indicated that he already has a father image associated with the helper. This father could become an intruder, a presence to deal with. The cousin may have had real trouble with his own father, a significant embodiment of the archetypal father, and he may shift or transfer that avatar of the archetype to you the innocent friend.

As a friend you could be either unconscious of this factor in your talking or, with a little education, you could recognize it. It always helps to know who and what you are dealing with. If it's the father figure that is nuzzling in on the conversation, you can spot him and deal with him accordingly. You could discuss your cousin's father and their relationship, sorting it out and bringing it into awareness. You could educate your cousin by showing him how this kind of intruder can interfere. Pointing out this otherwise hidden figure is itself a step forward in offering your cousin guidance.

In this example, you, the friend or concerned relative, also have to watch out that you don't unconsciously play the father in the way you relate. Entering the complex is not always a bad thing, but often it makes things difficult. You elicit many feelings from your cousin that have nothing to do with you but are leftovers from a relationship that may have been troublesome years ago. These patterns last a long time and come to life and complicate a current interaction.

I find that it is often better to remain neutral in the face of a wakened complex. You don't have to participate in it, but to be neutral you have to see it for what it is and keep your eye on it. Sometimes it won't go away no matter how neutral you are, and then you have no choice but to work it through with your friend or relative.

Jung said that a complex is like a separate person. When someone treats you like a father, you may have to assert your individuality. You could be a different kind of father or, better, a different figure in a different story altogether. In less common instances the person you are helping may be so locked into the complex that nothing you do has an effect. You may have to give up trying and suggest that your relative find someone else.

You have to respect the power of the psyche. I remember attending a workshop led by Rafael López-Pedraza, one of my most respected teachers of therapy, and he suggested strongly that there are times when you have to have the presence of mind to walk away from an impossible situation. If you can't walk away, then it is probable that you have an exaggerated sense of your own strength and ability.

Some intruders play a different sort of role that, as usual, can be both useful and problematic. For me, James Hillman, good friend and true mentor, sometimes makes life difficult for me now, eight years after his passing. He was one of those strong people who can so impact others that they allow him to enter their psyches and have his own room there. Jung has a similar impact on me, but not as much as Hillman and is not as present in me as much as he is in many of his followers.

There are certain terms, for example, that bothered Hillman. He complained about them often and loudly. One example is the word *experience*. He did not like people saying, for example, that we are "experiencing" good weather. He complained that we turn everything into an experience, focusing on ourselves rather than the object. He felt the same about *wholeness* and *personal growth*.

In this way Hillman is an intruder in my psyche. If ever I want to use one of these words, something in me shouts loudly, *Stop!* I am not the one objecting to the word; it is Hillman who has taken up residence in me. Sometimes I struggle with the intruder and win out in the end, using the offensive word. Sometimes I lose.

So when we are talking with people about serious matters, we have to discern who is speaking. I would say that much of the time, if not most of the time, it is an intruder and not the self speaking. Here I am not using the language of complex and transference. Instead, I am trying to be as concrete as I can be in showing what goes on in the psyche in our interactions. If we want to carry on a therapeutic conversation, which is a beautiful thing, then we could be more aware of the dynamics, personalities, and levels of narrative in play.

Therapy Is the Work of the Heart

For the umpteenth time let me say that the word *therapy* means care or service and not cure or fix. It is a matter of the heart, and what distinguishes a therapeutic conversation is the desire to care for another person in distress or someone trying to make sense of his or her life. *Psychotherapy* means, etymologically, care of the soul or soul care. Care is a heart term.

Whether you are doing professional therapy or being with a friend, you must be watchful not to take either the psyche (soul) or the therapy (loving care) out of psychotherapy. You can probably sense intuitively how soul and love go together, psyche and eros. Soul is intimate depth; love is intimate connection.

You may love the person you are caring for, or you may not. But in either case you can love their soul. I sit with a person trying to get along in a difficult life and I see the complexities, the adversities, and the struggles. I see them as the alchemy by which the person is trying to make soul out of a scattered life. I feel compassion for this basic human need to feel alive and to be a person. The struggle may make a person difficult to befriend or to like, but the soul-making is deeply human. I identify with the opus, the work of becoming somebody, and that love leads to care.

This means that your heart must be open and intelligently trusting and strong and secure. As a caring friend you have to be prepared for the challenges in your task. It is not always easy to care for a friend in emotional distress. You need to be somewhat stable and unshakable. You don't need to be superhealthy or perfectly composed. Your own struggles will help you deal with your friend's, and they will also keep the relationship tightly connected, not split into the healthy one and the sick one.

But you do need to be in touch with your strength, because your friend needs that. She does not need to know about your conflicts, and it's all right if she thinks you've solved all the problems. That fantasy about you could help her contact the source of insight and power within her. But you can't indulge in it, or the spell will be broken and it won't help either of you.

Do your best and don't be undone by any mistakes you make. Mistakes are part of the work, and if you don't make any, you would be quite suspect. Humans err. But a good friend is not discouraged by the mistakes he makes. He goes on doing his best to be a solid resource for his friend. He's willing to be the therapist of the moment, not a professional but a thoughtful human being who has something to give.

Now that you know you can be a lay therapist for your family members and associates, you can spread your wings and be a therapist for a needy world. Do anything you can imagine to contribute to the emotional health of the planet. All our troubles in nations and across the globe are psyche trying to find love and beauty. Few understand this, but maybe you do because of your experience with your friends. Bring that knowledge to our world and be a therapist who goes far beyond the professionals in your care for the soul of the world.

Let me finish with a few guidelines for friends counseling friends.

1. Don't think you know what your friend needs or who she should be.
2. Examine your own motives for helping, and clear your mind and will.
3. Don't think you know what is best for her.
4. Assure her that you can keep her secrets.
5. Listen closely to what she has to say and keep your solutions for another day.
6. Let her know that you have heard her.
7. Show her some real confidence and leadership.
8. Give her some genuine, positive feedback about herself.
9. Be devoted to her well-being and show it.
10. Notice any transferences, in you or in her, fantasies floating in the air and affecting the relationship.
11. Encourage her going further with stories that you sense are revealing and promising.
12. Show her strong friendship-love and support.

I am not a therapist
And yet I feel called to help
When my friend is grieving or confused.
Does my inner therapist have a license?
Is it all right to counsel my family members?
I go ahead and put out an invisible, metaphorical shingle
And practice with confidence.

REFERENCES

Berry, Patricia. (1982). *Echo's subtle body*. Dallas: Spring Publications.

Boer, Charles (Trans.). (1970). *The Homeric hymns*. Chicago: Swallow Press.

Campbell, Joseph. (1949). *The hero with a thousand faces*. New York: MJF.

Campbell, Joseph. (1988). *The power of myth* (Betty Sue Flowers, Ed.). New York: Doubleday.

Estess, Ted. (1974). The inenarrable contraption. *Journal of the American Academy of Religion, 42*(3), 415–34.

Euripides. (1973). *Hippolytos* (Robert Bagg, Trans.). New York and Oxford: Oxford Univ. Press.

Ficino, Marsilio. (1975). *The letters of Marsilio Ficino* (Vol. 1). London: Shepheard-Walwyn.

Freud, Sigmund. (1965). *The interpretation of dreams* (James Strachey, Trans.). New York: Avon.

Guggenbühl-Craig, Adolf. (1976). *Power in the helping professions*. Thompson, CT: Spring Publications.

Guggenbühl-Craig, Adolf. (1977). *Marriage dead or alive*. Zürich: Spring Publications.

Hillman, James. (1975a). Abandoning the child. In *Loose Ends*. New York: Spring Publications.

Hillman, James. (1975b). *Re-visioning psychology*. New York: HarperCollins.

Hillman, James. (1979). *The dream and the underworld*. New York: Harper & Row.

Hillman, James. (1981). *The thought of the heart*. Dallas: Spring Publications.

Hillman, James. (1983). *Healing fiction*. Barrytown, NY: Station Hill.

Hillman, James. (2007). *Mythic figures*. Uniform Edition (Vol. 6). Thompson, CT: Spring Publications.

Jaeger, Werner. (1943). *Paideia: The ideals of Greek culture* (Vol. 2). (Gilbert Highet, Trans.). New York: Oxford Univ. Press, 1943.

Jung, C. G. (1966). *The practice of psychotherapy*. Collected Works (Vol. 16). Princeton: Princeton Univ. Press.

Jung, C. G. (1968). *The archetypes and the collective unconscious*. Collected Works (Vol. 9). (R. F. C. Hull, Trans.). Princeton: Princeton Univ. Press.

Jung, C. G. (1973). *Memories, dreams, reflections* (Aniela Jaffé, Ed., Richard and Clara Winston, Trans.). New York: Pantheon.

Jung, C. G. (1976). *The symbolic life*. Collected Works (Vol. 18). (R. F. C. Hull, Trans.). Princeton: Princeton Univ. Press.

López-Pedraza, Rafael. (1977). *Hermes and his children*. Thompson, CT: Spring Publications.

Miller, Patricia Cox. (1994). *Dreams in late antiquity*. Princeton: Princeton Univ. Press.

Moore, Thomas. (1996). *The re-enchantment of everyday life*. New York: HarperCollins.

Moore, Thomas. (1998). *Dark eros*. Thompson, CT: Spring Publications.

Moore, Thomas. (2014). *A religion of one's own*. New York: Penguin/Gotham.

Rilke, Rainer Maria. (1984). *Letters to a young poet* (Stephen Mitchell, Trans.). New York: Random House.

Sardello, Robert. (1982). City as metaphor. *Spring: A Journal of Archetype and Culture*, 95–111.

Stevens, Wallace. (1989). *Opus posthumous*. New York: Alfred A. Knopf.

Suzuki, Shunryu. (1973). *Zen mind, beginner's mind*. New York and Tokyo: Weatherhill.

Thoreau, Henry David. (2013). *Essays* (Jeffrey S. Cramer, Ed.). New Haven: Yale Univ. Press.

Winnicott, Donald W. (1971). *Playing and reality*. London: Routledge.

Yalom, Irvin D. (2003). *The gift of therapy*. New York: Harper Perennial.

ACKNOWLEDGMENTS

After having been a therapist for forty years, I have many people to thank for the insights in this book. I will start with the several C. G. Jung societies, institutes, and analysts who have so generously invited me to speak and teach for their communities, even though I am not a registered analyst myself. This book also owes everything to my colleagues doing archetypal psychology, an important movement that not many know about. Those friends include James Hillman and Rafael López-Pedraza, who have passed on, and Patricia Berry, Robert Sardello, and Chris Robertson.

Constant friends who support me with an inspiring message at least weekly are Pat Toomay, a former pro football player and now wizard of the mysteries, and Brian Clark, one of the best astrologers on this planet. Conversations in London with Sarah Van Gogh have taught me how to expand my archetypal studies in a larger world.

My family gives me inspiration and ideas every day. Joan Hanley's wonder-filled paintings and penetrating thoughts keep me alive, and my daughter Siobhán's ideas in general and example in her field of music truly inspire me. My son by marriage, Abraham, an innovative architect, constantly expands my view of the world.

In the world of publishing I continue to be taught by my former agents Michael Katz and Kim Witherspoon and

Alexis Hurley at Inkwell Management, and now I enjoy the friendship and endless flexibility and advice of Todd Schuster. The trust and backing I received from former colleagues Hugh Van Dusen and William Shinker continue to make me feel optimistic in the current challenging realm of book publishing.

I want to thank Patrice Pinette for studying "healing words" with me with intelligence and warmth, and Gary Pinette for keeping me honest in general and for reading the manuscript of this book in an early form. My good friend Rev. Marcus McKinney, from whom I have learned so much, really helped with his spirited conversations about therapy as caring. He also read the manuscript and gave me helpful feedback. I appreciate the warm, expert, and steady support of Scott Neumeister.

I have been fortunate to have had remarkable clients in therapy over the years and especially as I was writing this book. Their generous and open hearts taught me once again that doing therapy is being in therapy. I won't mention their names because there is a chapter in this book on confidentiality.